Finding Abundance in Scarcity

Steps to Church Transformation

Edited by
Samuel Wells

CANTERBURY
PRESS
Norwich

© Contributors 2021

Published in 2021 by Canterbury Press
Editorial office
3rd Floor, Invicta House,
108–114 Golden Lane,
London EC1Y 0TG, UK
www.canterburypress.co.uk

Canterbury Press is an imprint of Hymns Ancient & Modern Ltd
(a registered charity)

Hymns Ancient & Modern® is a registered trademark of Hymns
Ancient & Modern Ltd
13A Hellesdon Park Road, Norwich,
Norfolk NR6 5DR, UK

British Library Cataloguing in Publication data

A catalogue record for this book is available
from the British Library

978-1-78622-369-2

Scripture quotations are from New Revised Standard Version Bible:
Anglicized Edition, copyright © 1989, 1995 National Council of
the Churches of Christ in the United States of America. Used by
permission. All rights reserved worldwide.

Typeset by Regent Typesetting

For the 84 people who had to leave
our staff team in 2020 due to redundancy
and for those whose initiative, efforts and generosity
have sustained St Martin's through challenging times

Contents

Preface

Abundance in a Time of Scarcity

SAMUEL WELLS

The Netflix series *The Crown* succeeds because of its writers' grasp of one particular aspect of storytelling technique. The secret is the interplay of cosmic event with intimate tenderness. One memorable episode, set in 1956, charts Elizabeth's personal concern that her husband is having an affair with a ballerina. Her public attention focuses on the emerging Suez crisis. The Suez crisis itself interplays international relations with a clandestine plot between France, Israel and Britain. Meanwhile Elizabeth's anxieties about her marriage are interwoven with her sister Margaret's traumatic search to land a suitable spouse. As the episode draws to a climax, troops begin their invasion while Elizabeth goes to see the very same ballerina at the opera house. The effect is exquisite.

Hans Urs von Balthasar describes this effect at length in his sprawling *Theo-Drama*. The intimate level is lyric: it's intense and passionate, but subjective and partial. The public level is epic: it's objective and wide-ranging, but detached and a little impersonal. When they interweave, the story becomes truly dramatic. If this process feels familiar, one simply has to consider the passion narratives. On an epic level, Jesus is dealing with the cosmic forces of sin and death and the political and religious powers of the day. On a lyric level he's immersed in the fragility of Peter, the perfidy of Judas, the passion of the woman who anoints him at Bethany, and the faithfulness of Mary and the beloved disciple at the foot of the cross. The interplay of the two, for example at the cry of dereliction, is what makes the scene so powerful.

I've never felt this power so much as in 2020. St Martin-in-the-Fields is a complex organization. It has a large congregation, by UK standards, and a significant public ministry, involving a good deal of broadcasting. It has a trading subsidiary (two cafés, a shop, and around 175 commercial concerts annually). It has a development trust and two homeless charities, one local, one national.

The pandemic asphyxiated its commercial activity, at a stroke deleting two-thirds of the congregation's income. At the time of writing, we have had to shed three-quarters of our commercial and ministry staff. It's been a devastating, depleting and distressing experience. Yet online, the congregation, its public ministry and its music have found a reach, purpose and dynamism like never before. All is made new. The musicians have recorded music, weekly, for 4,000 churches across the land. HeartEdge seminars have become a hub for innovation and evaluation. A new enquirers' course has drawn participation from people far and wide, a good many of whom were already inhibited by chronic illness before 'shield' became an intransitive verb. The national homeless charity has never been more in demand, or attracted more support, fervidly working to help people find secure accommodation.

The combination of these events has led to days of almost unimaginable contrast. In July 2020 all 125 employees of the business were told their roles were at risk of redundancy. Staff representatives described their colleagues' feelings and circumstances on frequent Zoom calls, as several of those same representatives were told their own roles are likely to go. Some staff members shrugged their shoulders and said, 'I've seen the news, and what's happening to my friends. I knew it was coming.' Others were totally blindsided that St Martin's could not somehow remain immune to the virus. Yet the same afternoon as one of the most difficult conversations, I led the first BBC Radio 3 broadcast of Choral Evensong for five months, an occasion that evoked a postbag of delirious gratitude. And that same evening I admitted 11 new members to our Nazareth Community, made up of people from all classes, including those who sleep outside, seeking the heart of God through shared practices centred on silent prayer. Founded two years ago, it has grown to 81 people, with an additional 36 online companions. It models the way we seek to see the assets in everyone, rather than regarding some as needy and casting others as benefactors.

It's been as if we are in a cartoon: on one side surrounded by footfall figures, government directives, church guidelines, protective equipment, and spreadsheets of redundancy calculations, earnestly trying to be humane, transparent and compassionate as we cast staff out into a wilderness of high unemployment and considerable health anxiety; on the other side surprised by joy, with people coming to faith, hundreds of thousands downloading choral offerings, asylum seekers stepping up to leadership roles, donors tendering generous gifts, and the church reopening in July for tentative public worship, only to close again in November and open again in December. In the background, intense discussions in which health and economics, the present and the future, caution and improvisation, hard-nosed fact and finger-in-the-air guesswork seem in impossible tension with one another.

Perhaps the bleakest day of 2020 was when all the pastoral, music and commercial staff were called to a Zoom meeting and we put everyone at risk of redundancy. After a relentless series of individual consultations lasting six weeks, followed by a second round some weeks later, I sat down to write 84 letters to those we could no longer keep on.

Doing so was distressing and humiliating. Humiliating, because I have spoken across the world about St Martin's, its vision and its business; and now the business was disintegrating before my eyes. Humiliating also, because we have such a grand reputation for caring for the destitute, but here we had no resources to care for ourselves. It was an experience of failure and powerlessness. To ask a middle manager to consult with and make redundant her whole staff team is really hard; then to say, I'm afraid you too will need to leave, makes you feel both cruel and impotent. I haven't felt I had the right to shed a tear, because others were materially affected so much more than me. But the last year has been about individual hardship, collective dismay and corporate impoverishment, and taking the three together has at times been overwhelming. I have nothing but admiration for the dignity and selflessness with which my colleagues left. I wanted to say to every one of them in the words of Isaiah 43, 'You are precious, honoured and loved.' But you don't say that to someone you're making redundant. So instead I said, 'You have been a blessing to this community, and those of us that remain are trying to work out how, without you, we can continue to be a blessing to others.'

But, beautiful things have been happening – too many to recount. Keep it quiet, but it's also been a complete nightmare, in which plans made and an institution crafted over generations have been torn apart in ways a raging inferno couldn't achieve. There have been moments when I've realized, 'I have no idea what to do or how this story can go on'; and the tears have been hard to suppress. And yet, like a ram in a thicket, something has been provided, or has emerged, or suddenly changed.

'It was the best of times. It was the worst of times.' Charles Dickens' summary of the French Revolution is a good fit for the pandemic at St Martin's. A child asked me, 'Did God create coronavirus?' I answered, 'I don't believe so. But God made the ability to change. Biologists call it mutation. Some changes are really bad ones, like this virus. But human beings can change too. And to get out of this hole, it looks like we're going to need to change a lot. Maybe for the better.' As always in ministry, the hardest thing is to take your own advice.

* * *

This volume is a humble account of how one congregation responded to the first eight months of the pandemic. It doesn't go into detail about the painful choices, dreaded conversations, ugly financial statements, multiple redundancies and extensive protective equipment. Instead it concentrates on a single notion: finding abundance in the scarcity of a pandemic. Clergy and laity at St Martin's have found beauty, truth and goodness in times of adversity, hardship and distress: enough to trust that their discoveries, humbly shared, may be of hope and inspiration to the Church more broadly.

I begin by setting a theological context, locating the pandemic as a time of exile in which, like Israel in Babylon, we may discover a truer face of God and a deeper sense of God being with us than ever before. The first chapter pursues similar theological themes through sermons that explore what's at stake in faith and action as the church has sought to respond to this challenge.

Chapter 2 follows the instant response of St Martin's in March 2020 to take its ministry online. Subsequent chapters explore how clergy and laity have sought to make the crisis an opportunity to go deeper and face truth: through contemplative prayer, in bereavement support, and in maintaining relationships with asylum seekers. The chapters that follow reflect the breadth of the ministry and mission of St Martin's – music, art, Scripture study, disability, expatriate support and prayer. Then two chapters describe the way the internet has fostered new community internationally, and a new way of coming to faith. Finally a conclusion and epilogue offer insight into how a strategy for putting such a response together might surface, and how the future church might accordingly be different.

This book has been put together by six clergy, two lay staff and one congregation member: but behind those who have written words down is a whole community – congregation, staff, volunteers, supporters, neighbours – whose business has long been improvisation in the face of opportunity, challenge, adversity and tragedy. There is no limit to what can be achieved as long as no one insists on claiming the credit. St Martin's is a community that thrives because no one is pausing too long to ensure they get the credit, which is why for so long it's been a place where remarkable things have happened. To the unseen, unrecognized, unthanked and unrewarded people who have made St Martin's thrive and helped it, in the face of genuine crisis, survive, this book is a small token of gratitude.

On 15 March 2020, as the tide of the pandemic was breaking in the UK, I began worship by saying the following words. I offer them here as the sentiment that has guided my own and my colleagues' ministry through the storm of these intense, distressing, but far from godless months. They were entitled, Something More Infectious.

We come to church each Sunday, we pray and read our Bibles through the week, to prepare ourselves. Jesus grew up in Nazareth, travelled around Galilee to prepare himself for Jerusalem. In Jerusalem people discovered who he truly was, and what his words and actions really entailed. We've spent decades, many of us, preparing we knew not what for. Well, now we know. This is the moment when the world finds out whether being a Christian makes any difference or not.

In Britain, we say pray for a sunny day, but take an umbrella. I'm not saying in the face of the virus we don't take sensible steps. We must follow public health advice. We do so not because others are a danger to us, but because we might, directly or indirectly, be a danger to them. We're a community defined not by fear but by trust, not by scarcity but by plenty, not by anxiety but by communion. It's time to show our true colours.

This is the moment to find ways to overcome isolation that don't involve touch. We have this opportunity to explore the hinterland of the word with, that doesn't always involve physical presence, but still means solidarity and kindness, generosity and love. We will limit our contact to protect the most vulnerable, but we still need to proclaim that there is something more infectious than coronavirus – and that's joy and peace, faithfulness and gentleness.

It was in its most bewildered hour that Israel in exile found who God truly was. This is our chance to discover what God being with us really means. None of us would for a moment have wished this crisis on anybody, let alone the whole world. But our faith teaches us that we only get to see resurrection through crucifixion; that we see God most clearly in our darkest hour.

Remember what Isaiah tells us. You shall cross the barren desert; but you shall not die of thirst. You shall wander far in safety – though you do not know the way. If you pass through raging waters in the sea, you shall not drown. If you walk amid the burning flames, you shall not be harmed. If you stand before the power of hell and death is at your side, know that I am with you through it all. Be not afraid, says our God. I am with you like never before.

This is our faith.

* * *

HeartEdge was founded in February 2017 on two theological principles. The first is that the people of God have tended to be closer to God in times of adversity than in periods of plenty. That's what the story in Daniel 3 tells us. If we are experiencing adversity in our church life right now, this is precisely the time we expect God to be close to us like never before. The second HeartEdge principle is that God gives the church everything it needs. But the church must be open to receiving that everything in the form God sends it: often those on the edge. We sometimes need help from one another to perceive where our abundant assets are truly to be found. Rather than bewail our scarcity, we need to sharpen our perceptions for the ways God is sending abundance. The name HeartEdge derives from the mission statement of St Martin-in-the-Fields: At the heart. On the edge. The heart refers to passion, faith, compassion, beauty, and the location of the church on Trafalgar Square, in the heart of London. The edge refers to St Martin's association with social exclusion, but also to the cutting edge of creativity and hope. The name HeartEdge recognizes that often the edge is found in the heart, and the heart is found on the edge.

HeartEdge's mission is 'catalysing communities of hope that reimagine church and society through the four Cs: commerce, culture, compassion and congregational life'. HeartEdge began with the recognition that a conventional church, committed to congregational life and compassionate outreach, but short on money and energy, and often numbers, could be revitalized in both by exploring commercial initiatives and developing cultural partnerships. That's been the experience of St Martin-in-the-Fields for the last 35 years, and it's a model we have been developing more recently with hub church partners around the UK and now on four continents. But what we have discovered in the last year is something different, though complementary. It's that when our business is paralysed, the other three Cs rally round to compensate. This is how we have found abundance at a time of scarcity.

Anyone familiar with the practices of improvisation in the theatre will recognize the impulses of HeartEdge. One is over-accepting. When an actor says 'no', or refuses to accept the premise of what's being said or done by others, it's known as a block. When an actor says 'yes', and inhabits the implied story proposed by others' words or actions, it's called accepting. But here's the crucial thing: there's a third option. Overaccepting means fitting the smaller story of what's in front of you into the larger story of God. The most obvious example is the cross. Jesus doesn't block the cross – he doesn't escape; neither does he accept the cross – passively yielding to his fate. Instead, he overaccepts the cross. In his resurrection he takes the rejection, cruelty and death into himself and makes them part of a greater story. On an even grander level, God does not block Israel's faltering embodiment of the covenant; neither does God simply accept it: in Jesus God overaccepts the covenant and opens it out to the whole world. Once spotted, this move can be discovered everywhere in the Bible. It's the secret of almost all the stories told in this book. It's the heart of HeartEdge.

The second improvisatory practice is reincorporation. At the end of a Dickens novel or Shakespeare comedy, the characters reassemble on stage, and unresolved antagonisms or misunderstandings are reintroduced and addressed. This is an image of what Jesus calls the kingdom of God. In the kingdom, the neglected, lost and rejected reappear as a gift. Jesus' ministry reassembles the outcast, the scorned and the discarded and embraces each as a person with a role to play in God's future. At the end of the feeding of the 5,000 story, the disciples collect up 12 baskets of leftover food – an act of reincorporating that anticipates the way, in God's kingdom, nothing is wasted. Jesus' words, 'The stone that the builders rejected has become the head of the corner', outline the way his own reincorporation after rejection by his people heralds manifold forms of subsequent reincorporation of those thought to be outside God's promises. This is the edge of HeartEdge.

The pandemic has been a ghastly nightmare we wouldn't wish on our worst enemy. But I hope the ways we at St Martin's have been shown abundance in scarcity will inspire you to recognize the same pattern of overaccepting and reincorporation in your own settings. These aren't big-budget initiatives born from carefully crafted strategic plans: they are all on a shoestring, from an organization with no reserves in the bank. They aren't clever, spontaneous ideas in a vacuum by ecclesial entrepreneurs: they are practices emerging from the logic of what we were already doing, and from the angels God sends us. It hasn't been happy; but there have been ways in which the Holy Spirit has made it beautiful. Best of all, as John Wesley said in his dying breath, God is with us.

Introduction

A Theological and Pastoral Framework

SAMUEL WELLS

Here I offer three addresses, all given on Zoom, one to clergy colleagues in central London, a second to the Festival of Preaching, and a third to the Duke Divinity School community. The first offers a theological framework, the second a devotional one, the third a pastoral one. Together they offer a suitable introduction to the chapters that follow.

Meeting God in the exile of lockdown: Daniel 3.8–30 (12 May 2020)

I wonder if you feel like an exception. You look around you on Zoom, Facebook, Twitter, and you see churches ploughing through lockdown, being renewed online, having a good war, seeing God do new things and true things every day. But inside, a part of you thinks, 'I'm different. It seems to be Boomtown Rats for the upbeat and energized, but it's not working for me. Don't tell anyone, but I put my sermon online and it got three engagements and an average viewing time of 20 seconds. Don't let on, but I'm feeling completely deskilled and paralysed right now. Don't dwell on it, but there's been such a huge row in my household overnight that I can't even concentrate sitting here on this call right now.'

I wonder if one of those is you. I wonder if every one of us is an exception.

If so, we're in good company. The Bible is full of exceptions. If you're a minority, imagine being in Babylon during the Jewish Exile. If you're feeling like God's forgotten you and you've been written out of salvation's script, try being transported a thousand miles and living without all the signs of God's presence – land, king and temple. The book of Daniel is about obscure people, faraway people, exceptions, those who don't fit the script. And yet they trust in God. It's a story about a people who lost their home, lost their hope, lost their security, lost their families, lost their heritage, lost their land, lost their story ... and found God.

Could that be us? Let's find out.

Nebuchadnezzar is God. That's what we're supposed to think. That's why he has satraps, prefects, governors, counsellors, treasurers, justices, magistrates, and on and on. He's got so many staff it takes a whole day for them to march past. He's so up himself that he makes an enormous golden statue, a great vast pillar in the sky – nudge nudge – and everyone has to bow down and worship it when he clicks his fingers, or rather when he clicks his horn, pipe, lyre, trigon, harp and drum. Anyone who doesn't is thrown into the blazing fire. Shadrach, Meshach and Abednego are having none of it. Their story shows us what salvation means.

What salvation *doesn't* mean is that we're not going to get the virus. Salvation doesn't mean freedom from sickness, care, anxiety, fear, pain or threat. Shadrach, Meshach and Abednego don't avoid the fiery furnace. Christians don't believe they are immune from suffering, sealed off from worry, aloof from conflict, inoculated against panic, exempt from grief, vaccinated from the virus. Quite the opposite. As this story makes clear, Shadrach, Meshach and Abednego face suffering, worry, conflict, panic and grief precisely *because* they are people of faith and *because* they uphold God's name.

What salvation *does* mean is one of two things. This story shows us both of them. When Shadrach, Meshach and Abednego are thrown, bound, into the fire, *God is with them*. There aren't *three* figures walking in the flames; there are *four*. My guess is every single person on this call has seen or at some time owned a small picture of footprints walking across a beach and an inscription that explains that for a stretch there was only one set of footprints because for that part of the journey Jesus carried you. It's a pious sentiment but I'm not sure it's what Christians call salvation. What Christians call salvation is what we see in this story. *Jesus is with us in the fire.* The destiny of Shadrach, Meshach and Abednego is settled not before they reach the fire by some stunt that makes them avoid the flames; nor is there any dramatic rescue from the flames. Their salvation takes place *in* the flames, as they discover Emmanuel: God is with them *in* the flames. Our salvation is the same. Here's the bad news. God doesn't spare us from the fire. God doesn't rescue us from the fire. Here's the good news. *God is with us in the fire.* 'Though I walk through the valley of the shadow of death, I fear no evil; for you are with me.' 'When you walk through fire you shall not be burned, and the flame shall not consume you.' That's the gospel.

I believe this is the single most important story for understanding the Old Testament and how it came to be written. The fire represents Babylon. Shadrach, Meshach and Abednego aren't spared from the fire, nor rescued from the fire; they find they are *with* God in the fire. Somehow the fire is a fire not just for them but for God too. The same is true for Israel in Babylon. Israel isn't spared exile. Israel isn't rescued from exile. Israel finds in exile that *God is there too.* The appearance of the fourth figure in the fire sums up the experience of exile for Israel. God is *with* us. That's salvation. Exile is the place Israel wrote down the Bible. Exile is the time Israel found it was closer to God than it had ever been in the Promised Land. Exile is the crucial motif for shaping our response to the virus. Exile was the lens through which the early Christians came to understand Jesus' death. Jesus has his own fire, which we call the cross. Jesus isn't spared the cross. Jesus isn't rescued from the cross. Jesus is *with* God on the cross. The bonds of the Trinity are stretched to the limit; but not, ultimately, broken. When we see the cross we see that God is with us, however, whatever, wherever ... for ever. This is our faith.

But that's not all that salvation means. There's a second

dimension. Shadrach, Meshach and Abednego *do* emerge from the fire. But look how it happens. They are called out by Nebuchadnezzar! See how God works. We want the dramatic intervention miracle. We want God just to spirit the virus away. What we get is conversion instead. The embodiment of pride and cruelty, the Babylonian king becomes the one who calls Shadrach, Meshach and Abednego from the flames. There's no Christianity without conversion. We can talk all we like about people of good will; but see how salvation works through conversion. Nebuchadnezzar was the agent of imprisonment, punishment and trauma, and he becomes the means of deliverance, transformation and restoration. That's called conversion. And how and why is Nebuchadnezzar converted? Nebuchadnezzar sees Shadrach, Meshach and Abednego and sees that God is with them; and because God is with them they feel the force of the flames but the fire has no final power to damage them, distort them, destroy them. That's called being a Christian. We feel the force of sin and suffering, we're stricken down by sin and suffering, but, because God is with us, the virus has no final power ultimately to damage us, distort us, destroy us. That's our ministry. That's our witness.

I wonder who Nebuchadnezzar really is. I wonder if there's been such a person or power in your life, dominating, oppressing, threatening, hurting. I wonder what it's like to go into the flames. I wonder what it's like to feel that whatever that Nebuchadnezzar has done to you, in Jesus, God is with you, and nothing Nebuchadnezzar can do can damage, distort or destroy you. I wonder what it means to imagine Nebuchadnezzar's conversion, and the hope that all your grief and suffering and exile and this terrible virus will one day be redeemed, and become part of what we call the gospel. I wonder what it's like to realize you're a Christian.

The centre of the story is what Shadrach, Meshach and Abednego say to Nebuchadnezzar. I challenge you to hear these words this afternoon without trembling. 'If our God whom we serve is able to deliver us from the furnace of blazing fire and out of your hand, O king, let him deliver us. But if not, be it known to you, O king, that we will not serve your gods

4

and we will not worship the golden statue that you have set up.' Hear those words echoing through your ministry in this pandemic and from this moment forward.

Shadrach, Meshach and Abednego are speaking to a sceptical king. Sceptics aren't our enemies. They draw out of us what we truly believe. We all have sceptics in our own families – the truculent father-in-law, the rebellious daughter, the person we love who doesn't share what's most important to us. Lockdown time is open season for sceptics. Sceptics say things like, 'Jesus expected the imminent end of the world. But it didn't come. So why should we believe the rest of the things he said?' You know that if the end of the world had come the Church wouldn't have written the New Testament, and if it wasn't for the New Testament, we wouldn't know anything about what Jesus did or didn't think or say or do. But what you say is, 'The end of the world may yet come. *But even if it does not*, we will trust the incarnation and ministry and death and resurrection of Jesus as the foundation stone of everything that we know.'

Sceptics see how self-absorbed the Church becomes, submerged in internal questions like when to open churches or how to celebrate communion online, and sometimes oblivious to those who are hardest hit medically or economically. Sceptics say things like, 'If Christianity's true why doesn't it make us better people? Why are Christians so mean and unfaithful, greedy and bigoted?' You know Jesus dies because of our sins. We never forget we have sins enough to make Jesus die. The gospel is about forgiveness, not about never getting things wrong. But what you say is, 'Christianity may make us better people. *But even if it does not*, we will trust that God in Christ has come among us as the truth and in the Holy Spirit has made it possible to see and know the truth today.'

But in the face of the virus you will be less concerned with sceptics than with people you have come to love who are facing agonizing suffering or distress, who call or FaceTime you and say, 'Where is God now?' You're talking to a vulnerable person, who has overheard frightened relatives sharing hushed whispers of fear, and yet is bombarded by people who seem to think their job is to keep cheerful and so ensure it may never happen. And this person calls you, because you're the only one who has the courage and the faith to tell them the truth. And they say to you, 'Am I going to die today?' And you say, 'Your doctors hope you might get through this. *But even if not*, God is with you in your last breath and God will not let even death destroy you. Neither death nor life can separate you from the love of God, dear one.'

Or maybe you're actually doing that strange thing, making time between Zooms to speak to an old friend, and your companion says, 'D'you think she'll ever come back? D'you think she has any idea how much I love her? D'you think there's anything I can do to get through to her?' And you see the screen tremble, and you realize it's because your companion's gripping their desk for dear life because there's nothing else in the world to hold onto. And you say, 'I hope she'll come back. *But even if not*, know that God will never leave her alone; and God will never leave you alone. And even in the fire, where you are right now, God is making something beautiful out of your lonely, broken heart.'

But your ministry isn't all about others, what they think and how they feel. Your first job in ministry is to save your own soul. And there may be people on this call who have flourishing ministries, healing neighbourhoods, nations, even the Anglican Communion, meanwhile pausing to brush up their medieval Latin and rewrite the *Summa Theologiae*, stay one step ahead of popular electronic devices, and take a whole youth programme online while still doing pizza and sleepovers in lockdown. But you may be here this afternoon realizing that your heart and soul doesn't lie in career and public profile but in rearing children and being a friend and neighbour; or that as far as understanding where you belong in the kingdom of God lockdown has left you none the wiser, albeit better informed. And I say unto you, 'Maybe you'll flourish in ministry in the years ahead; maybe you'll look back on this season as a time of renewal and your sense of call will be honoured and fostered by disciples and overseers alike. Maybe every day you'll wake up and again feel a freedom in God's service that surpasses any other possible joy. *But even if not*, know that God is redeeming the world through your hands, your feet, your heart, your love, your gentleness, your kindness, whether you're aware of it or not.'

Or maybe you're on this call thinking, 'Perhaps I'm the only person here whose faith is fragile, whose prayer life is a bombsite, whose lifestyle is unrecognizable as Christian, who just can't seem to find God anywhere near a church. I feel like the ultimate exception.' Well if so, you're a gift to everyone else here, because there isn't anyone who at some moment in the next 30 years won't be sitting where you're sitting today. To go through life without the fire (or the refrigerator) of doubt may sound like being a priest; but it doesn't sound much like being a human being. I say unto you, 'Maybe you'll know God's presence every hour, every breath, every touch. *But even if not*, know that God is with you in every moment of the universe's existence. You may believe and trust in the living God. *But even if not*, the living God lives for you.'

We all know that most beloved verse in the Scripture, 'God so loved the world that he gave his only Son, so that everyone who believes in him may not perish but may have eternal life.' But we also know that, if it was that simple, we wouldn't need the rest of the Bible. The poignancy of what Shadrach, Meshach and Abednego say to Nebuchadnezzar is finally not just what we say to a sceptic, or to a person in pain, or to ourselves, but what the members of the Trinity say to one another. When Jesus goes to the fire, when Jesus faces the flames of hell for us, when Jesus hangs on the cross, what does he say to the Father? Is it so different from the words of Shadrach, Meshach and Abednego? 'If you will deliver me from the cross, O Father, then take this cup away from me. *But even if not*, be it known to you, O Father, that my love for you will hang on for ever, and that those who somehow find that they have lost you can hang onto me.' Isn't that what makes Jesus' final words so wondrous? Jesus loves us so much that he goes to the cross even if there's no certainty of resurrection. Jesus isn't just keeping his side of the bargain. Jesus is loving *even if not*. That's the definition of love.

We've come face to face with God. We've come to the foot

of the cross, the heart of Jesus. We've come to the definition of love. It lies in those four little words: *But even if not*. Those words are the heart of God. Make them your response to this virus. Make them the centre of your faith. Make them the heart of your love. Make them the whole of your vocation. In them you will find God. *But even if not*, in them, God will find you.

Prepare six envelopes: Luke 11.1–13 (29 September 2020)

Prayer is our duty and our joy. You could divide the Church into those who pray because they believe it's their duty, and those who pray because they're expecting it at any moment to become their joy. Perhaps the most basic Christian prayer is the Lord's Prayer, because Jesus said, 'Pray in this way ...', thereby making it easy for us. But here's the paradox. Jesus said, 'When you are praying, do not heap up empty phrases as the Gentiles do.' But for those of us who are in the habit of saying the Lord's Prayer once or twice, perhaps three times a day, how does it not thereby become the heaping up of empty phrases?

Here's an honesty session. In the last six months, have you experienced fear, despair, paralysis, denial, confusion and frustration? Has prayer seemed at the same time more useless and more necessary than usual? I'm assuming your answer to both questions is yes. What I want to do today is to rediscover the Lord's Prayer in the midst of this distressing time. Maybe it seems the prayer is not enough. I want to explore with you how the Lord's Prayer is actually plenty – in fact, more than enough for such a time as this.

OK, here we go. It's the morning after the Brexit vote. David Cameron clears his office at Number Ten. He leaves on his desk, for his successor, three envelopes. Beside them he places a note: 'Open one of these when you get into trouble.' Fast forward a year. Negotiations with the European Union begin. Theresa May opens her first envelope. It reads, 'Blame your predecessor.' A year later, she loses the first vote on her Brexit deal. She opens her second envelope. It says, 'Do a cabinet reshuffle.' Six months later, she loses the third vote on her Brexit deal. She opens the third envelope. This is what it says: 'Prepare three envelopes.' It's not known how many envelopes Boris Johnson has so far opened.

The pandemic has changed very little. But it's intensified almost everything. What it's intensified more than anything is our deepest fears. We have all kinds of anxieties in our lives. But they boil down to two. One is this: 'Am I living a purposeless existence in a pointless world in a meaningless universe, which is, however, full of urgency and demand – yet will eventually revert to nothing?' That's the grand-scale anxiety. The second is this: 'I feel so vulnerable, so fragile and so alone, and life could go down the plughole at any moment.' That's the micro-scale anxiety. These two fears stalk our lives. I wonder whether, alone in the night, you ever think, 'If I actually stopped my frenzied activity, constant communication and perpetual distraction, and actually thought about one or other of these anxieties for any length of time, the panic would be uncontrollable.'

How do we deal with these two anxieties? There are two conventional ways. Fervid busyness; or perpetual diversion. They are really the same; and together they simply create a different form of anxiety. What the pandemic has done is to reduce our options for busyness and our avenues for perpetual diversion. That's why we hate it so much. So what other options do we have?

There is a way. We've been given a gift. It's a very tiny gift. But it's also an indescribably huge gift. It's 70 words long. And we can recite it several times a day – in fact as often as anxiety strikes. It takes as long as the guidelines say we should wash our hands. That gift is the Lord's Prayer.

The Lord's Prayer appears in slightly different form in Matthew and Luke's Gospels, and when we say it today we add on some extra words about the kingdom, the power and the glory that actually come not from the Gospels but from 1 Chronicles. So today I'm going to talk about the version we're familiar with, minus the additional part. I want you to think of the prayer we know so well as actually like six envelopes that Jesus leaves on our desk, any or all of which we can open when anxiety strikes. Imagine Jesus getting ready for the ascension and saying to Peter, 'Back in the upper room I've left six envelopes. You might want to think about opening one of them when the Church gets into trouble.'

Let's start with the first three envelopes. They address our first anxiety: 'Am I living a purposeless existence in a random world in a meaningless universe?' We'll take each envelope in turn. Here's what's written in the first envelope: 'Our Father, who art in heaven, hallowed be thy name.' What does this tell us? It tells us there is, actually, a purpose: God wants to be in relationship with us. There is one who is in another realm from us, a realm infinitely more real than this one. Who yet relates to us not as an impervious despot or cynical manipulator but as a parent. It tells us there's something bigger and more significant and more real than the universe: which is called heaven. If only God lasts for ever, and what lasts for ever is the only thing of absolute value, everything in our lives is valued according to how much it relates to God. To say 'hallowed be thy name' is, at a stroke, to reappraise the value of all our commitments, our projects and our desires. Just like that.

A month ago I walked past my old school. I looked into my first-year classroom, which had changed disturbingly little. It took me back to when I was 11 and I took a test in that very classroom. In italics at the top it said, 'Read all the questions.' Then it provided 12 questions, about all sorts of trivial things. 'Spell rhododendron backwards.' 'Calculate the score of the alphabet if A=1, and B=2, and so on.' The last question said, 'Put your pen down and don't answer any of the questions.' Which made all of us in class feel foolish, because none of us had followed the instructions. We had answered all the questions, which we wouldn't have had to do if we'd read all the questions. Only the last question made sense of all the others. The Lord's Prayer begins with words that make sense of everything else. God is beyond everything, yet seeks relationship with us, and we must prize this truth above all else. Simple, yet staggering. That's our first envelope.

Let's open the second envelope. Here we read these words: 'Thy kingdom come.' Only three words. But so full of significance. We know now God wants to be in relationship with us. 'Kingdom' says what relationship means. That full quality of healthy encounter – with God, ourselves, one another and creation – is what God has in store for everyone and everything. We long for a world in which justice is done, mercy is shared, goodness is honoured, cruelty is ended, selfishness is dismantled, and kindness prevails. 'Thy' is a warning. It tells us that until God finally brings that full expression of healthy relationship, we will continue to live under other forms of kingdom, whether of others' devising or of our own. Some of these may be bad, others not so bad; but whether bad or good, they aren't God's kingdom.

I bet you've got your own checklist of how the world would be so much better if you were in charge. It's hard to say, 'Thy kingdom come' and renounce the desire to say, 'My kingdom come.' A lot of people have been convinced that all would be well if only they were in charge. Stalin, Trump, Kanye West. Few if any have been proved right. And then there's the word 'come'. 'Come' tells us that the kingdom is something God brings, not something we achieve. It's great if our efforts align with and anticipate that kingdom; but that kingdom isn't primarily about affirming us. It's about saturating the world with the glory of God. That's our second envelope.

Are you ready for the third envelope? This is what our third envelope says: 'Thy will be done on earth as it is in heaven.' God has given us freedom. We can use that freedom to depart from God's ways or to seek God's ways. It's not that the universe is meaningless and our lives purposeless; it's that there are multiple possible directions of travel, and our own will is part of that mix. But we're seeking to discern, discover and direct our lives in the trajectory that will ultimately prevail. This envelope also delivers us from any idea that all that matters in life is being ready for eternity. It longs for God's will for formed and restored relationships to be experienced on earth now, just as much as they will be enjoyed in heaven for ever. The way to prepare for heaven isn't to withdraw from earth and bide our time till we can be fully with God. It's to recognize what full, true and restored relationships with God, ourselves, one another and creation look like. And it's to do whatever we can to seek that such relationships pervade our bit of earth right now. Build new and good ones; restore and heal bad and complex ones.

I don't know if you've ever used a Magimix to chop and blend food for a recipe. Sometimes it feels like you have to put the parts together a hundred different ways before suddenly it all goes whizz and is done in seconds. Our lives are a constant searching for the 'whizz' that is finding God's will. But be careful about searching for God's will. You may find it. And once you do, you may find the living it harder than the searching for it.

This is the hardest of the six envelopes sincerely to pray. If you speak to a monk or nun about their vows of poverty, chastity and obedience, they will tell you that the first two aren't as tough as you would think. The really hard one is obedience. There's only one thing worse than not getting what you want – and that's getting it. There's only one thing worse than not knowing God's will for your life and that's knowing it. Then you have no excuse not to live it. Be careful what you pray for.

Together these three envelopes address our first anxiety. This is what they tell us: God longs to be with us and will finally pervade both earth and heaven. These three envelopes shape our hearts after the heart of God.

Now for the second set of envelopes. The first three envelopes are all about God; the second three envelopes are all about us. They address our second anxiety, 'I feel so vulnerable, so fragile and so alone, and life could go down the plughole at any moment.'

Here's the fourth envelope: 'Give us this day our daily bread.' 'Give us.' It's in the present tense. It's about now, today. There's one question that haunts the Old Testament. Will God be enough for Israel? Sometimes God is too much – too holy, too demanding. Sometimes God seems too little – too distant, too little help in trouble. In the Old Testament, bread is always about manna. Manna was a gift from God to prove to the Israelites that, even in the wilderness, God would provide for them. But it was also a test, to see if they would be content to collect just a daily amount and not try to get enough for the next day too. And in the New Testament, bread is always about the Eucharist. It's always about believing God has given us enough by giving us Jesus; or striving for more – which turns out to be less. This is the great question for us too, never more than in a pandemic: is God enough for us? Sin is always a sign that for a moment, a day or a lifetime, God doesn't seem to be enough – so we go chasing our security somewhere else. 'Give us' is the fourth envelope: a request that God will be enough.

Here's the fifth envelope: 'Forgive us our trespasses, as we forgive those who trespass against us.' If 'Give us' is about the present, 'Forgive us' is about the past. Which scares us the most? The past, which will come back to haunt us, or the future, which is full of unknowns? There' are two painful things about the past: the things done to us, which leave us bitter; and the things we've done, which make us guilty. We want justice for the first set of things, so we can be vindicated; but we fear justice for the second set of things, lest we be condemned. 'Forgive us ... as we forgive' is telling us we can't have one without the other. Justice shaped by mercy for the first yields mercy shaped by justice for the second. Together they are telling us we can't live in the present unless we and God take steps to heal our past. Be careful when you call for justice; because one day, justice may call for you.

And here's the sixth and final envelope: 'Lead us not into temptation; but deliver us from evil.' Temptation is about the things we think we can manage but get bigger on us. We think we can fit them into our story but it turns out we become part of theirs. We become trapped by them. Evil is something that threatens to engulf us. We know we have no power to resist it. Only God's protection can deliver us from evil. Our lives are dominated by anxiety about the future – the things we can anticipate, like temptation, and the things beyond our imagination, like evil. This is a prayer to be free from the fear of the future. At Christmas 1939, George VI quoted the words of

Minnie Haskins. 'Go out into the darkness and put your hand into the hand of God. That shall be to you better than light and safer than a known way.' 'Lead us not ... Deliver us.' This is saying to God, 'You have provided for our present and healed our past. In the future, be with us always.'

That's the second set of envelopes. They are about the present, the past and the future. If we are healed of our past and freed from our future, we can truly live in the present. These three envelopes show us what salvation means.

That's all the envelopes of the Lord's Prayer. It turns out it's not a heap of empty phrases. It's 70 words that speak into our deepest fears, and beside those fears set the deepest truth there is. If you're saying you're someone who never thinks, 'I'm living a pointless life in a meaningless universe', and who never worries, 'My life is only a heartbeat away from falling apart', then I'm saying, quite simply, I don't believe you. But if you're surrounded by fighting within and fears without; if you're living through a pandemic, struggling to believe that God is enough, yesterday, today and for ever – then hear this good news. God has prepared for you six envelopes, and left them on your desk. They are the only advice you need. Open them. Open them not just when you're in trouble. Open them not just when anxiety knocks at the door. Open them every day, several times a day, as often and for as long as you wash your hands in a pandemic.

This is what they say. God is with you. God is coming to you. God will finally prevail. God gives you enough for today. God heals the hurt and damage of yesterday. God will be with you for ever. Whatever happens.

That's it. Do we need anything beyond that? I don't think we do. That's enough. That's plenty. Actually, that's more than plenty: that's everything we will ever need.

Soul-tending in a virtual age: how to preach, pastor and disciple in these challenging times (Duke Divinity School, 16 November 2020)

The pandemic has forced the Church and its clergy to ask and face fundamental questions about who we are and what we are trying to achieve. My hunch, and this is a tough thing to say, is that we find the constraints and demands of the pandemic tiresome, but what really gets us down is having to face these fundamental questions relentlessly. In my remarks today I'm going to start by outlining what I believe these fundamental and deeply uncomfortable questions are. I'm then going to offer six beatitudes of lockdown that seek to realign our imaginations from the incarceration of lockdown to the joy of salvation. And in my final section I'm going to speak specifically to the practices of preaching, pastoring and discipling in a virtual age.

Fundamental questions

I suggest that the pandemic raises three fundamental questions, which in each case have a wrong answer and a better answer, and in each case we do anything in the world not to ask, but which in fact direct us to the truth about discipleship, ministry and mission.

Here's question one. What's the matter? In other words, what's the thing that's so wrong right now? *There's a very infectious and sometimes fatal disease.* OK. There have always been diseases and maladies. *But a lot of people are dying.* OK, but we all die eventually. Death is universally infectious and always fatal. *But the measures taken to avoid the disease are constraining.* OK, but every life is bound by constraints. In the end all of us have to find ways to come to terms with and dwell within our constraints, rather than always assume we can overcome them. *But these constraints dismantle our economy.* OK, but we've always had periods of economic contraction and hardship. *But it's affecting some people terribly, in impoverishment and mental anguish.* OK, but hasn't being with people in times of distress and despair always been the Church's calling, and isn't the more widespread prevalence of adversity a cause for renewal of that calling? *But it feels like God's abandoned us.* Aha. Now we're talking. I think this is the heart of it. We had a package that if we were faithful in ministry and our people were adequate in tithing and our denomination succeeded in not splitting over sexuality then God would reward us with bounty in this life and harps and clouds in the next. Good deal. Remind me where it says that in the New Testament. Or is it in the Book of Discipline?

I'm going to sound very harsh and pastorally insensitive, but there's nothing about the pandemic that we didn't sign up to when we were baptized, that those called to ordination didn't agree to when they became a pastor. I say to my colleagues, when the parishioner emails to say their loved one's desperately ill, or the funeral director calls to say there's been a death, or a lay leader texts to say, 'I've just been fired,' there should be a part of you inside that leaps up and says, 'This is what I was ordained for. I get to sit with these people in the abyss of unknowing and the tremble of fearing and the horror of losing. We look down as far as we dare into the fathomless depths and we trust that if we look down far enough we'll see not nothing but the face of Christ.' That's the heart of our calling. And the pandemic just means that we get to do that with a whole society, a whole world, all at the same time. Isn't that a fantastic privilege? Isn't that the most important thing in the world?

Here's question two. What is church? Here's my favourite definition. Church is the body of Christ – the fully human, fully divine place where divinity and humanity meet, most explicitly in the incarnate Jesus, but derivatively in God's people, shaped by baptism, renewed by the Eucharist, empowered by the Holy Spirit, the place of reconciliation between heaven and earth, between essence and existence. It is not the full embodiment of Jesus Christ, nor is it the complete fulfilment on the last day – but in the meantime it is the physical and spiritual bearer of who Christ is and what it means and entails to be in full communion with him. Is any of that seriously impaired by the pandemic? No, I don't think so either. So what's the problem? Well, there's a second definition of church. Church is the local manifestation of those seeking to inhabit this vision; it exists as a congregation of faithful people in which the pure Word of God is preached and the sacraments duly administered. It's a group of people doing their best to live with each other under God. And there's no denying that it has had to adapt, in pretty much every congregation in the world. Social distancing, hand-sanitizing, livestreaming: we've all had to learn new tricks this last eight months. But surely, even in that second definition, we're still a group of people doing our best to live with each other under God. Aren't we?

Or has church come to mean something rather different? Something about habit, in which the routine of Sunday worship service and adult ed class and Wednesday night Bible study and vacation Bible school and church council budget meeting grinds on inexorably regardless of how far or near it is from the kingdom. Something about place, in which this particular building, where a special person's funeral happened and a more complex person's wedding took place, where children were shaped and friendships were fostered – this place is the focus for hopes and dreams and memories and truth. Something about permanence, when everything in life seems fragile and transitory. We've had most or all of that ripped away or transformed beyond imagination. But isn't that an opportunity for rediscovery of which parts truly were infused by the Holy Spirit and which parts existed because the last pastor was a bit of a control freak and her predecessor a bit lazy? Isn't the reason we are struggling so much with the pandemic not that the money's dried up and we don't know how to pay for everything but because we've been forced to see things in a new light and we wonder if half the things we thought we needed to pay for are actually inhibitors rather than conduits to the kingdom?

Here's question three. What is a pastor? At this point I'd forgive you for stepping off the Zoom call because it's getting too close to the bone. I'll tell you, in case, in the stress and confusion of the pandemic, you've forgotten. The Church is not the only way the Holy Spirit is active making Christ present in the world. But the Church is the most reliable and definitive way in which we find our collective bodies shaped into the body of Christ. And the most time-honoured way this happens is through prayer, the Eucharist, baptism, Scripture-reading, pastoral care and preaching. Which is why the Church sets aside specific people to become so proficient at those things, and so adept at enabling others to make those things the framework of their lives, that the rest of the Church can relax and know those things are in safe hands. But pastors are human, and both they and the Church sometimes lose confidence in some or all of these things, or their ability to perform them well. So instead we substitute being frantically busy and always stressed and much in demand and never able to be fully present with anyone. Because that's our definition of important, and that's our way of never having to identify priorities or disappoint anyone's projections.

And would it be cruel to say that the problem with the pandemic is that we haven't been able to be frantically busy and we haven't been allowed to hide behind being always stressed and we haven't truthfully been in much demand? So we have had no excuse not to be fully present with suffering people and hungry souls and empty hearts. We've got very excited about regulations and guidelines and got exasperated about inconsistencies and incongruities, all as a distraction to feeling useless and powerless. But in fact we've been given the greatest opportunity of our lifetimes to be pastors: to rediscover our core identity and to exercise our unique calling by doing some very simple things very well.

But to do so may require a change of heart and soul and mind and strength. Which is why we need some beatitudes.

The beatitudes of lockdown

Blessed are you who expect God to be more intimately revealed in exile; for you shall behold the risen Christ. The Old Testament was written down in Babylon, as Israel came to a new understanding of who God was, and discovered that God was more with them in exile than ever before in the Promised Land. The early disciples likewise realized that they had seen the face of God more truly in Christ's crucifixion than ever before. If you speak to an ordinary Christian they will not say, 'Jesus was with me when my daughter rampaged through the national championships before going on to Olympic glory.' They will say, 'I was by my mother's side in hospital and I felt an urge to say the Lord's Prayer and I saw her lips quiver when it came to the power and the glory, and then by the time we got to Amen she was gone, and I felt the Holy Spirit lift her life up and bring her home.' Anyone who thinks life is about routine and comfort and security has got the Bible and 2,000 years of the Church's experience to contend with. Remember Martin Rinkart who, having buried his whole family in the Thirty Years War, heard of the Peace of Westphalia and sat down and wrote 'Now thank we all our God'. This is where to find God. Are we looking?

Blessed are you who find abundance in scarcity; for God will give you everything you need. I'm not the first to point out that if you're in lockdown and you go outside early in the morning, you see some things unchanged by the pandemic: behold the birds of the heavens, they hoard not, neither do they panic-buy; consider the lilies of the field, they fret not, neither do they lament. But you also become aware of other things transformed by the pandemic – there is no aeroplane noise, less traffic, and the air is much cleaner. More subtly, concern about people's well-being means we check in with friends and family more often. We reach out to neighbours whose names, if we're honest, before March we could never recall. We join initiatives of solidarity in the neighbourhood that until now we never had time for. Listen to what the Spirit is saying to the churches.

Blessed are you who do not valorize one historical or cultural manifestation of being church; for you will never be in a straitjacket. I tend to the view that arguing over whether the person watching on livestream is in full communion with Christ, even if they don't themselves receive the transformed elements of bread and wine, is fiddling while Rome burns. The point is that the Church in the West is falling over itself to write poems about its own decline. We've been given this one-year, or maybe three-year, period of grace to experiment with and try out myriad forms of worship and pastoral care and fellowship to evaluate which ones are of lasting value and can be incorporated into our future normal. What a gift. Don't you ever think the disciples who attended the Last Supper would look at our battles about styles of music or arrangement of pews and laugh at us before they started to cry in disappointment and bewilderment? We're being given a glimpse of an alternative world. It's a time of testing and discerning. It's not permanent. How can we not receive it as an opportunity?

Blessed are you who are hungry for God's grace; for you will find and recognize it in the strange forms in which it comes along. The pandemic has necessitated new partnerships, catalysed new connections and forged new friendships. For example, at St Martin's our local Sikh restaurant saw my colleague Richard Carter talking about our asylum-seeker ministry on television news and offered to supply 50 curries a week, which they are still doing. It's only when you recognize your own fragility and know your need of God that you're ready to realize that what's coming towards you is an angel rather than a threat. God gives the Church everything it needs, even in a pandemic, but it takes two to tango: the Church has to be willing to acknowledge that God might come in the form of a Sikh, or, perhaps more mysteriously, in the form of a Christian who believes differently on some of the issues of the day.

Blessed are you who realize that incarnation happens in the world as it is; for you will find relationship anywhere. There's a part of every Christian that secretly thinks it was a lot easier for the first disciples. Jesus called them, they spent a lot of time with him, they knew what he was up to. But the Gospels present the disciples not understanding about the feeding of the 4,000, believing they were perishing on the Sea of Galilee, and fleeing at Jesus' arrest. There is no ideal, and at the same time no obstructively unpropitious circumstance for appreciating incarnation. The world we currently experience as deprived and desultory is indescribably privileged compared to the world of any preceding century, and the highly developed world is still extraordinarily affluent compared to the two-thirds world today. I've never fully understood what F. D. Roosevelt meant by the phrase, 'We have nothing to fear except fear itself,' but he went on to refer to 'nameless, unreasoning, unjustified terror which paralyses needed efforts to convert retreat into advance'. I think he meant you get what you come looking for.

Blessed are you who believe the future is always bigger than the past; for you will always be excited by what God is doing next. In Romans 13.11 Paul reminds us that 'now is our salvation nearer than when we believed'. Perhaps the biggest heresy of the mainline Church today is an assumption that it once got things right, and that it did so in the 1950s. Yes, that's right – the hopelessly racist, sexist, imperialist and McCarthyist fifties. That was the kingdom of God back then – didn't you realize? Christians don't believe in progress; but neither do they believe in decline. What they do believe is that our past is healed by forgiveness and our future is held in the palm of God's hand – so there's nothing to fear. Yes, we should be grateful for what our forebears achieved, but let's not be intimidated by it. The joy of the gospel is certainly what God has done, but is just as much what God is doing, and is most of all what God will do. I worry that our present lament was already almost fully formed in almost all its dimensions before the first case of Covid-19 arrived on our shores. God is with us – was fully with us in Christ, and will be fully with us for ever. Ain't that good news?

How to preach, pastor and disciple in this challenging age

Once we have faced the most challenging questions, and allowed our hearts to be reshaped and our souls reoriented by beatitudes, we can find the freedom to preach, pastor and disciple in this challenging age. Let me say a word about each one.

What matters about preaching right now is not that we're doing so online, but that we're doing so in the midst of a global crisis. A global crisis is always likely to become a heresy – by which I mean it's likely to make us think it's more real than the gospel. The thing to get right about preaching is not the camera angle, or the use of a script or not, but to make sure every time you're speaking your words from the very depths of what you believe. The crisis threatens to saturate the imagination. Your job as preacher is to tell a story more compelling, offer a narrative more intriguing, and paint a canvas more thrilling than the one coming out of CNN and Fox News. That doesn't mean offering an op-ed every Sunday. Some days it means making no reference to politics, social unrest or public health at all.

What you're saying is that there is something more infectious than coronavirus – and that's the wonder that in Christ for ever has become incarnate in today, so that our today may be transfigured into for ever. Just make sure you say it in the right tone of voice. It's not strident and conquering. It's faithful and gentle. It doesn't need backing vocals. It just needs to be shared as if it were the last words you were ever going to say. You shall cross the barren desert; but you shall not die of thirst. You shall wander far in safety – though you do not know the way. If you pass through raging waters in the sea, you shall not drown. If you walk amid the burning flames, you shall not be harmed. If you stand before the power of hell and death is at your side, know that I am with you through it all. Be not afraid, says our God. I am with you like never before. This is our faith.

As to being a pastor, it's not that we have no way to do it – it's that we have more ways to do it than ever before. If you haven't mastered Zoom, Teams, Skype, FaceTime and WhatsApp video, there's always a much-neglected tool that we used to call the telephone, or text or email, or letter, and if everything fails there's driving round to someone's house and talking to them from beyond their window or front door. And for a pastor it's never just a question of how can we get to talk – it's always just as much a question of am I the right person, and can I connect you with someone who is more local to your neighbourhood, able to resist your bewildering charms, sympathetic to your repetitive grievances, or less at risk from the virus than I am. But the gift of the pandemic is that it's taken away the veneer of small-talk and made it perfectly legitimate to start the conversation by saying, 'Are you frightened?' The chances are the response will be, 'I break out in a sweat ... I find myself overcome by anger ... I wake up in the night ... I get panic attacks.' You're concerned, but not surprised. And isn't that exactly what a pastor should be – concerned but not surprised? You're making your worship, your conversation, your parish activity spacious enough for people to explore what they're going through, deep enough for them to trust it's real, true enough for there still to be hope. Isn't that what you went into this for?

And finally discipling. I'll tell you a secret. It's actually easier on Zoom. When you're asking people to talk deeply about their experience, to explore honestly about their fears and convictions and to listen intently to what you want to share, it just works better when participants are in the comfort and security of their own homes. It's one of the ways we find abundance in the midst of scarcity. The internet means that people find you who never normally would – some of them shut in their homes long before the virus struck. And if you create bridges for them to walk across, you're likely to find them more receptive than at almost any previous time in their lives. You've just got to have a gospel that takes their experience very seriously, indeed more seriously than they do, as a lifetime of encounter with the Holy Spirit, and you've got to have a confidence that Christ is generally more present or at least more tangible in adversity than in prosperity.

I'm not saying anyone would welcome the pandemic or wish it on their worst enemy. But I am saying there is no good reason why this can't be for the Church a time of growing deeper, refining our mission, and rediscovering our foundations. Don't worry about what you do or don't do with your smart phone, for just a moment. Concentrate on what we're told about the still, small voice. And make sure that when that still, small voice pipes up, you're not distracted by the paraphernalia of protective equipment or livestreaming. Instead, you're listening.

Finding God in Lockdown

SAMUEL WELLS

This chapter offers a series of sermons I gave at St Martin's in the early months of the pandemic. The stated texts and dates give a sense of the way thought, faith and reflection progressed. The sequence ends on the day the congregation re-entered the church in July 2020. Of course that's not the end of the story; but perhaps the end of the beginning.

But this I know: John 9 (22 March 2020)

We seem to be living in a science-fiction film. Humankind is facing a collective threat unknown in our lifetimes. And withstanding it requires a level of social and international cooperation that's putting a huge strain on everyone.

The current crisis is affecting all of us. But perhaps most painful is the way it's affecting each of us differently. For some of us, catching the virus is a profound discomfort; for others, it could prove to be fatal. Some of us are simply trying to keep sensible distancing guidelines; others are at real risk, working in intensive care and emergency wards. Some of us have incomes that are secure; others could find ourselves impoverished by business shutdown and economic downturn. Some of us feel busy and urgent, making a difference in people's lives with new arrangements and complex plans; others feel utterly powerless, embarrassed that what seemed so important and necessary a fortnight ago seems so trivial and irrelevant in the present crisis. Some of us are taken up with the daily tasks of getting groceries and medicines; others have had our lives turned upside down by cancelled exams, postponed weddings, impossible choices and enforced separation from loved ones. Some of us complain of inconvenience and criticize overreaction; others are overwhelmed by having to work and still care for children, the fragile routines of life disintegrating before our eyes.

On a personal level, what's most bewildering is how much of what we now have to do goes against our deepest impulses. We want to be present to one another, shake hands, embrace, put a kind hand on a shoulder; but all this is now unwise and irresponsible, if not to us, then to them and to third parties. We want to gather, be in solidarity, offer practical help and real companionship; but we find in the immediate term we show our care for the vulnerable by discouraging encounter and by keeping people away from each other. We believe isolation is humanity's biggest problem, because if we come together, between us we have all the skills and resources, wisdom and experience we need: but right now things are so bad that we have to practise isolation for an even more pressing good – our health and our concern for one another's safety, even survival. It's dismantling so many of the good habits we have long sought to foster in one another.

On an existential level, it keys into our deepest fears. We cannot escape to a part of the world that isn't affected. We cannot see an end point when we'll be able to relax and put it behind us. It's dangerous, and still getting bigger. It's invisible, universal, unstoppable, and currently without cure. There's only one thing anything like it – and that's death itself. And that's the worst thing of all. The virus is a premonition of our own death – shutting down communication, depriving us of companions, relentless in its march towards us, all-consuming in its imminence and slow inevitability.

But that realization – that our response to the virus anticipates and models our attitude to death itself – provides the clue to how we are to think about it now. When people want to discredit Christianity and religion in general, they often say, 'It's just an elaborate way of dealing with the universal fear of death.' To which I say, 'Yes, and are you going to tell me you have a better way?' The crucial point is, if we can find a way to stare down our paralysis and anxiety in the face of death, nothing can finally hurt us. We become the most powerful people in the world. No one can threaten us, intimidate us, blackmail us, derail us; because the ultimate threat isn't a threat to us.

Of all the verses in the Bible, one stands out for me. It's from Song of Songs chapter 8. 'Set me as a seal upon your heart, as a seal upon your arm; for love is strong as death.' Here's the deal about Christianity, when all the complexities of life and faith and church and experience are stripped away. Christianity is the conviction that love is stronger than death, and that if we are sealed upon God's heart we need not be afraid; not now – not for ever. Christianity is the trust that on the cross Christ sealed us upon his outstretched arms: and in Christ's resurrection God showed us that love is stronger than death. The love of the Trinity is ultimately unbreakable, and is the very core of all things, and if we love too we shall be part of that everlasting, unbreakable love. The cross shows us that such love includes terrible grief and pain and even despair; but the resurrection shows us that such wondrous love will ultimately prevail. Right now we feel the love of the cross in all its agony and dismay more than we feel the love of the resurrection. But one day we shall discover that the two loves are the same love, and nothing can separate us from that love.

The hymn 'I cannot tell', written in 1929 by the Baptist leader William Young Fullerton, gives us an appropriate shape for how we may live in the face of Covid-19. Fullerton structures his convictions around the tune *Londonderry Air*. The tune has four lines of wistful and sometimes sorrowful lament, followed by four lines arising from the ashes of bewilderment, inspired by the words, 'But this I know'. I want now to offer a version of Fullerton's hymn for such a time as this.

I cannot tell why grief and sadness linger
Why jobs are lost, and people face despair;
When this will end, if vaccines come and rescue,
Why fear and sickness tremble in the air.
But this I know, Christ feels the hurt upon the cross;

The Spirit weaves our lives together still.
And some glad day, through Providence, the Father
May turn this wave of loss to glory by his will.

I cannot tell how we can be together
When all our ways of doing so are lost;
How we can be one body in communion
If every form of touch comes at a cost.
But this I know, we're sealed upon the heart of God
The Spirit dwells within our fearful souls.
And Christ finds ways to show his face to all of us
To lift our hopes and make our broken spirits whole.

I cannot tell how long this time of fear will last
If there'll be months, or years of wilderness;
When once again we'll gladly throng together,
To sit and laugh, to dance and play and kiss.
But this I know, we're finding things both good and true
About our God, each other and our homes.
So after this we'll know we've met our darkest hour
And now there's nothing we will have to face alone.

What we don't know is daunting. But what we do know is
beyond glory. The hardest part, day to day, is to keep our perspective wide, so we recall, in the trials and challenges of each
day, that we are living on the broad canvas of eternity, and
that God created the world to be with us, and will never leave
us alone. If we live or if we die, we are in Christ. Everything
changes; except the thing that matters most.

I haven't forgotten it's Mothering Sunday. I want to finish
with a thought about a rather old-fashioned word. Mother-
hood, in most but not every case, is closely related to giving
birth. And all of us are very glad that someone went through
this strain and sometimes agony to bring us into the world.
In days gone by, people would refer to the last stages of preg-
nancy as confinement. The curious thing is that confinement in
a different sense is exactly how many people are experiencing
this virus. Confined by not being able to be close to friend and

colleague. Confined by having no money to spend. Confined by being forced to stay at home. Confined, with the illness, by being stuck in bed, or in hospital.

The insight we get from this double meaning of the word confinement is that the agony of childbirth is the prelude to the single most wonderful thing about life: and that's the miracle of birth. Confinement means a period of strain and distress and extreme pain that yields endless life and energy and wonder. In the midst of our sadness, suffering and bewilderment today, maybe we could think of this time like a child in the womb, growing in hidden ways, drawing on unknown resources, discovering our true identity and preparing for what is to come. This is Mothering Sunday: the day we recognize the cost of confinement. But also the day we remember the paradox we first knew as babies ourselves: that confinement is not the end of life as we know it, but its hidden beginning.

Three kinds of resurrection: John 11.1–45 (29 March 2020)

One of the major changes in education in the last generation is the greater awareness of various learning styles. Diversity isn't just about identity and conviction; it includes the way we learn. The educationalist Howard Gardner devised a sevenfold scheme known as the multiple intelligence theory. He speaks of *visual* learners, who tend to go into engineering or design; then *aural* learners, who are good with speech and music; then *verbal* learners, who go for journalism or politics; *physical* learners, who go for PE or emergency services; *logical* learners, who find numbers easy and head to accountancy or computer programming; *social* learners, who head towards HR or coaching; and *solitary* learners, who become authors or researchers. There's a huge discourse of people questioning aspects of these distinctions or the whole theory. But the point is, a given lesson in a classroom or presentation at a conference is going to suit some people more than others, and we each have to adapt to gain knowledge and understanding through the routes that work best for us. It would be dull if we were all the same, and we can help each other with complementary learning styles.

If that's how our intellect works, how much more our emotions. Our emotions aren't shaped just by dispositions of our heart and soul; they're conditioned by our life experience. When we enter a new situation, we judge it by its merits: but we also quickly assess whether it reminds us of a scenario we've been in before. Sometimes this assessment is subconscious, and it's only much later we realize why we found a person's voice frightening or flinched when we saw a cat. Some of our reactions are down to personality, but many are derived from conscious or unconscious memories of good or bad encounters in our past. There are way more than seven kinds of experiences, so no one has seriously tried to map out the range of different reactions people can have to the same situation. But you'll have cried all the way through a film while your companion remained utterly unmoved. And when you heard a person cry out in the street you'll have leapt down the steps to help while your companion remained rooted to the spot. It could be because you're compassionate while your companion is heartless. More likely it's something rooted in your respective memories.

And that connects to what we've been witnessing in the last week, as our national life has changed beyond description. In a lot of ways we're all in the same boat – not just in Britain but across the world. But what being in that boat means to us differs in myriad ways. Because some of us are anxious about our health, others distraught about our finances, others angry about being deprived of a much looked forward to event or much prepared for exam, others terrified about being cooped up with people they don't trust, others getting in touch with profound fears about being alone, isolated, forgotten, abandoned. And we react in different ways – some hyperactive, organizing everything and everyone, ordering or buying vast supplies for a two-year lockdown; others passive, mesmerized by graphs of death rates in European countries or hoping a magic fairy will make it all go away.

I want to look at the story of the raising of Lazarus in the light of this sense that our respective emotional and experiential make-up is different, and we react in different ways to the same things. The story has a background and a foreground. In the background of the story lie the disciples. Their reactions provide the context of Jesus' actions. They have three kinds of reactions. The first is fear. Jesus says, 'OK, guys, we're heading back to Judea.' The disciples reply, 'Last time we were there they were trying to stone you; you can't be serious about going there again!' Then they move from fear to complacency. Jesus says, 'I'm going to wake Lazarus up.' The disciples respond, 'If he's asleep, he'll be fine.' Then from complacency they move to martyrdom. Jesus says, 'We're going, like it or not.' Thomas says, 'Let's go and die with him.' Again, see how these three reactions map onto the emotions stirred by the virus these last two weeks. Fear, complacency and courage. Some are paralysed by fear. Others are blasé and can't see how the problem affects them. Others are heading towards the problem, going daily into hospitals, putting their own safety to one side, just wanting to be of help and support to the sick and dying. That's the background.

But in the foreground we have two figures, Martha and Mary, who react to Jesus in very different ways. I want to look closely at how their reactions to their brother's death can mirror but also guide our own reactions to the virus.

Let's start with Martha. Quickly she asserts herself as the outgoing, proactive member of the family. Martha goes out to meet Jesus as he comes to Bethany. You can see how conflicted she is.

I remember saying to a passionate colleague years ago, 'Your emails always charge in right in the middle of your stream of thought, saying, "We can't let so and so treat us like this – we've got to tell her to back off." How about starting a message by saying, "I hope you're well. I'm imagining this is a busy time for you," or some way of recognizing the person reading the message isn't immediately in the same place you are?' Martha sounds like my former colleague. She plunges in. 'Lord, if you had been here, my brother would not have died.' Just ploughs in, taking for granted her agenda is everyone's agenda, full of reproach that Jesus wasn't to hand when needed. And then she stops herself, realizes she's in a conversation, and changes tune. 'But I know God will give you whatever you ask.' Feel the passive aggression in that. 'You couldn't be bothered to be here. And now you could fix all this if you were interested. But I know you won't. Because you aren't.' We say the cruellest things to those we love, especially when they have gifts we know we'll never have. Martha's devastated. What she can't see is how anyone could feel differently from her.

Jesus pulls rank. 'I am the resurrection and the life.' Then he challenges Martha. 'Are you on board with this or not?' Martha says, finally, 'Yes, Lord. Everything I believe about God has come true in you.' See what's happening here. Faith can mean belief – that's to say, convictions held in the head. But it can also mean trust, a relationship that involves the heart. Martha first articulates belief, but then speaks words of trust. 'It's you – all this has become true in you.' Then Martha has one more challenge. She's moved from head to heart. But she hasn't yet got to hand. Jesus says, 'Take away the stone.' Martha is revolted. The horror overwhelms her. Jesus asks, 'Do you want to see the glory or don't you?' Finally Martha acquiesces. She wants to see the glory. Whatever it takes.

Let's turn to Mary. Bereavement turns Martha to activity. But it turns Mary to depression. Mary doesn't come out to greet Jesus. That's not an accidental detail. That's a sign that Mary's in a really dark place. Losing her brother means she's lost her household income overnight. There's no government support for small businesses whose boss just died. She's facing poverty. Martha comes back to get some sense into Mary. 'Jesus is here and wants to talk to you.' Mary comes to Jesus and parrots exactly the same words as Martha has just said. 'Lord, if you had been here, my brother would not have died.' But unlike Martha, Mary doesn't correct herself. It's like she has said these words to herself over and over, and now she says them out loud. That's actually the only thing she says in the whole story. Her silence speaks louder than any words. She's speechless with sorrow.

Martha and Mary both exhibit signs of profound grief. Martha is angry, demanding answers, eager to be active but still with her no-go areas. Mary is depressed, incapable of find-ing words. Maybe we recognize either Martha or Mary, or a bit of both, in ourselves and in those with whom we've spent the last ten days, domestically or virtually. But see how both sisters, and their dead brother, are swept up into the glory of God by what happens at the end of this story. Martha, who feels let down by Jesus, and demands more, finds far more than she had imagined. Mary, who had lost all hope, finds that Jesus will come to meet her deepest need even though she has no energy to respond. And Lazarus, who is the other side of the stone in the stench-filled tomb, has the greatest transformation of all. The plight of all three siblings is real, and at the start of the chapter seems irreversible. But Jesus changes everything: assertively for Martha; gently and compassionately for Mary; decisively and miraculously for Lazarus. See how there are three resurrections in this story. Resurrection from a broken relationship; resurrection from depression; and resurrection from death. What they have in common is this: Jesus changes everything.

Whatever our learning style, we all love a good story. And this is the greatest story of them all. We're like Martha, Mary and Lazarus – troubled, lost and dying. God seems so far away. Jesus comes to us, at immense risk to himself. He meets us, whether we're angry or depressed. He comes to our place of greatest fear, grief and fragility. He faces that place with simplicity, compassion and strength. And he raises us for new life with him, now and for ever. That's John chapter 11. That's the gospel. That's the whole Bible.

Wherever we have been this week, beyond Judea, feeling far away from the action, in Bethany, amid the tears and grief, or at the tomb, facing the stone of our horror and terror, we've got a place in this story. It's true that almost all of this story is made up of distress and despair. But just look how it ends. Just look how it ends.

It's how our story will end too.

Three dimensions of resurrection: John 20.19–31 (19 April 2020)

I'm guessing that most of us wake up in the morning with the thought, 'This can't be happening: this lockdown, this perpetual house arrest, this orchestrated nothingness is some kind of prank that everyone's playing one me. It's not real.' Then we go into a kind of paralysis, overwhelmed by the global size of the problem, the seemingly endless and obviously inadequate plan for overcoming it, and our own powerlessness to change the reality around us. Sooner or later, in seconds or hours, when the pillow has failed to provide the escape we deeply seek, we turn to the tasks of the day, humble or grand, onerous or pleasant, by which we break down the impossible into the humble, the unassailable into the simple, the daunting into the achievable. Three levels of waking up: denial, depression and resolution.

Albert Camus' 1947 novel *The Plague* is set in the town of Oran in French-occupied Algeria in 1948. The action takes place in the late summer, as bubonic plague sweeps the town, causing it to be sealed off. As the population faces danger, disease and death, the novel studies the reactions of various characters as the situation becomes more desperate.

The central character is Bernard Rieux, a doctor in his thirties. He's the first to diagnose the plague, and he sets up a hospital to treat patients. The tragedy and grief get to him, and he suppresses pity and withstands tiredness through pragmatic resilience and dogged perseverance. In contrast to Dr Rieux is a smuggler called Cottard. Cottard comes to life as the plague strikes. It's clear that he operates best in times of danger and suspense. He cashes in on the crisis, spiriting away those who wish to flee the town and selling illegal cigarettes and alcohol. When the plague abates he loses his mind and starts shooting people randomly from his balcony. A third character is a Jesuit priest, Father Paneloux. He preaches sermons that say the plague is a punishment and the death of an innocent child is a test of our trust in God. He joins the volunteer workers resisting the plague and dies soon afterwards.

Finally there is a playboy called Jean Tarrou and a journalist called Raymond Rambert. Tarrou is jolted out of his wealthy, idle ways by the onset of the plague. He establishes the teams of volunteers and is among the last to die, seeking to become a saint, even though he doesn't believe in God. Rambert tries to escape the city when the plague descends, using Cottard's smuggling network. But he has a change of heart and joins the fight against the plague, recognizing that a private happiness in the face of others' suffering is no true happiness at all.

Through these five characters the plague reveals who we are and displays how we respond. The plague is a time of judgement and revelation. Dr Rieux shows pragmatic determination, but at the cost of human feeling. Cottard is a cynical manipulator, but his gains are only short term. The other characters make and find meaning more successfully in small gestures of kindness than in grand claims about truth.

Camus turns out to have written an extraordinarily prophetic book about the 2020 coronavirus pandemic. People in 1947 thought it was a critique of the French capitulation to the Nazis in 1940 and the subsequent occupation. But it turns out it was about events that didn't take place till 73 years after it was written. Just as in the novel, we find in ourselves and those around us the same three levels of response to the virus. Some doggedly plod on through it, bravely doing what must be done, medically or economically, putting feelings to one side and incurring a huge personal toll. Others exploit or manipulate the situation, finding personal gain in the distress of some and the despair of many. And in between lie many who don't know what to think or how to behave, captivated one moment by thoughts of sanctity, another by armchair philosophizing, another by longing for escape, and eventually dragooned into solidarity finding we're all in this together.

Camus' novel shows us a world without resurrection. Whether living for themselves or for others, each character embodies an existence without hope. Even the priest speaks of a distant God making judgements and setting tests without tenderness or passion. What the novel deftly describes is how the same event can be interpreted differently by a variety of people, so much so that it's almost a different event. That insight gives us an important interpretative tool for understanding Jesus' resurrection.

The story of Thomas seems originally to have concluded John's Gospel. The sentence or two that follow it sound like they are wrapping up the whole story. John 21 seems to have been added as an epilogue. You can see why the Thomas story was considered a fitting conclusion to the Gospel when you look at the three dimensions of resurrection the story shows us.

The first dimension is political. When Thomas says, 'My Lord and my God!' he's using a title, in Latin *Dominus Deusque*, habitually accorded to the Roman emperor. It's common for Christians to refer to God, or more specifically Jesus, as Lord. But it's less common for Christians to realize that in doing so they are making a political statement. I don't think right now our political leaders are too bothered if the odd Christian says, 'Christ is my master in all things,' as long as we pay our taxes and keep two metres away from each other. But in a totalitarian state like the Roman Empire, you could be executed for less. Thomas is saying, 'If you've been crucified by the Romans and have been raised, you are my leader.' In a way we don't often dwell on, Jesus' resurrection is a dethroning of the Roman Empire and a transformation of all allegiances. Resurrection is political.

The second dimension is cosmic. Thomas is quite right to tell the other disciples he doesn't believe them. We would be just the same as him. They're asking him to suspend his whole understanding of how life and death work. They're challenging him to believe that the most crushing disappointment in their lives has been reversed. He thinks it's a cruel joke. It's an illusion, simply wish-fulfilment, a hallucination born out of grief. When Jesus appears and invites Thomas to touch his hands and side, it's not just a restoration of Thomas' relationship with the disciples. It's a transformation of everything that today we would call science. If a person can rise from the dead, anything is possible. That's the point. If crucifixion can't separate us from God in Christ, nothing can. If death can't bring Jesus' story to an end, death won't bring our story with Jesus to an end. Resurrection is cosmic.

The third dimension is personal. This is the part we relate to most easily. Thomas has a chance none of us get: he sees the nail marks; he touches the wounds. He speaks with the risen Jesus. Around 200 years ago Christianity changed. It changed because the eighteenth-century Enlightenment had convinced educated people that the grand quasi-scientific claims of faith were unsustainable, and that the public claims of faith led to endless conflict. So Christianity reinvented itself as a personal experience – something out of the reach of science or political manipulation, that was just about me and my God. We've already seen that the Thomas story is saying that this is non-sense. Jesus' resurrection was political and cosmic from the word go. But it's also personal. It's also about experience, relationships and trust. It's about Thomas touching Jesus, and seeing in him something beyond the wildest dreams of Galilee and the shattered hopes of Calvary. Resurrection is personal.

The crisis triggered by the coronavirus has many levels to it. It's medical, most obviously, because in the absence of a cure or even a vaccine it's pushing medicine to the limits of its capability. It's political, increasingly, because the best balance between limiting the spread of the virus, sustaining the global economy, limiting individual freedom and putting countless people at risk of poverty is almost impossible to achieve. And it's acutely personal, for those most at risk, for their carers at home and in hospital, and for everyone whose life has been turned upside down.

The virus has confronted us with a transformation of reality on multiple levels. It has revealed our characters and demanded our response. It has shown us that the same reality can look different depending on what kind of person you are, and where in society you find yourself. But the story of Thomas is challenging us to believe that there is a reality larger, deeper and truer than the virus. That reality operates on political, cosmic and personal levels. It meets us every which way.

The virus is telling us a political story of chaos and confusion. Jesus' resurrection is showing us a political story of confidence and solidarity. The virus is telling us a cosmic story of death and meaninglessness. Jesus' resurrection is showing us a cosmic story of being touched by Christ and being with God for ever. The virus is telling us a personal story of anxiety and despair. Jesus' resurrection is showing us a personal story of trust and faith.

The true plague that stalks us is not a physical contagion. It's an infection that impoverishes our notion of power, limits our concept of God and dismantles our ability to trust. That infection didn't start with the virus. It's been around a good while. When Jesus meets Thomas a week after Easter Day he transforms our perception of power, expands our understanding of God and restores our capacity to trust. He meets us on every level. He's above, beyond and outside our imagination, our limitation and our comprehension. He's our Lord and our God.

Essential journey: Luke 24.13–35 (26 April 2020)

When you're looking in at Christianity from the outside, it's easy to see the Bible as full of stories of faraway people of which we know nothing. It all seems obscure and distant. In 1777 the philosopher G. E. Lessing crystallized this problem in a memorable sentence: 'Accidental truths of history can never become the proof of necessary truths of reason.' In other words, a story is just a story; it's full of particular details that have no essential bearing on the truth about existence. What Lessing didn't realize is that everything is part of a story. Even when we give a rational or mathematical explanation for something, we are assuming some kind of a story. Stories are the way we join different pieces of information together to make a coherent whole. Right now, in the midst of the virus, we have no idea how to do that. The reason we're so perplexed is that we have no idea what kind of story we're in, how long it is or where it's all going.

When you look at Christianity from the inside, the stories of the Bible feel completely different. Rather than assume our story is normal and these stories are weird, we start to think the other way round. We come to regard them as our story, and we find meaning and truth by locating our story within their story. Rather than think our story makes sense and these stories are nonsense, we realize how incoherent is our story and how our stories only begin to make sense when we allow this story to become our story.

I want to tell the Emmaus road story with this transformation in mind. In the simplest sense, it's the story of two people whose story made no sense until they let Jesus tell them his story, and then they were on fire with a true story. Let's walk through it stage by stage and see how that transformation takes place.

At the start, the disciples' story makes no sense. When Jesus asks them their story, they open their mouths, but no words come out. 'They stood still, looking sad.' Stay with that description, for a moment. If Jesus were to come up beside you and your companion, and say, 'Tell me what you're discussing,' would that be you? 'They stood still, looking sad.' Hard to blame them: they'd invested their whole lives in Jesus, they'd risked their necks, they'd left their work, they'd invested in him their whole meaning and purpose. And he had been crucified. They were shell-shocked. Is there a part of you that is stationary and sad? Paralysed and frozen? Numb and lost? Here you are, in this story.

Then Jesus coaxes the story out of them. It's a cascade of words and events. Until the one that matters. 'We had hoped that he was the one to redeem Israel.' Pause again, and put the most shattering event of your life into that space. 'We had hoped ...' That covers it. See how the word 'hope' contains a story. When a child dies, you grieve what you have known; but even more, you grieve the years that never came to be. 'We had hoped.' When a relationship ends, you mourn the loss of something special: touch, laughter, companionship; but even more, the seizing away of something you glimpsed, the folly that for a moment you dared to dream. 'We had hoped.' When a political leader is assassinated, you fear an upsurge of violence; but you lament the future that seemed to be opening up, the new beginning snuffed out. 'We had hoped.' Here you are, in this story.

Then something remarkable happens. Jesus has heard the two disciples out. He has waited gently beside their silence, and listened patiently to their story. What he does next is to tell a story that doesn't deny their story but envelops it in a larger story. He embraces their feelings and their facts and encloses them in something more expansive and more wonderful. 'Was it not necessary...', he says. 'Was it not necessary that the whole purpose of creation was for God to come in person and be with Israel in flesh and blood? Was it not fitting for the covenant on tablets of stone to turn into a covenant of flesh and blood? Was it not inevitable that when divine goodness came face to face with human frailty, humanity would regurgitate and annihilate it?' 'Was it not necessary' doesn't have to mean that God planned it all. It means that God found a use for it all. Nothing could finally resist being folded into God's story. 'Was it not necessary': you've been there. It's the moment when you scatter the broken pieces of your story out in front of you, and then someone gently and kindly but inspiringly puts them together in a coherent shape like a mechanic assembling a motorbike from items strewn across a garage forecourt. Was it not better that you knew what heartbreak felt like, so when joy came along you realized how precious it was? Was it not necessary for you to experience failure, so you could become a compassionate person who understands that life isn't fundamentally about winning? Was it not necessary? Here you are, in this story.

The disciples don't want it to end. They spilled out their story and it was sad and stuck. This is the same story, but in Jesus' mouth it's amazing and glorious. 'Stay with us,' they say. Oh, how we know that feeling. I could have danced all night and still have begged for more. We don't want it to end. We've met a very special person and we want to go on talking and grafting our life into theirs for ever. Who cares if the train has reached the station, the course is over, the music has stopped. 'Stay with us.' We want more. This is fabulous. But think about it. We can't freeze the frame. You can't put a moment in a bottle and keep it for ever. We all know people who want their marriage to be like their wedding day, want their Christian life to be like their conversion, want to turn a rolling film into a static photograph. We know that instinct very well. 'Stay with us.' Here we are, in this story.

'Then their eyes were opened.' Everything suddenly made sense. There was only one explanation. Perhaps as they saw Jesus break the bread they beheld the nail marks in his hands and they realized they were sharing the body of Christ, the Eucharist, as the body of Christ, the Church, in the presence of the body of Christ, the risen Jesus. Their story and Christ's story fell into place. Mystery became reality, grief became joy, companionship with one another became camaraderie with God. Their eyes were opened. In a flash, you looked at an old friend, and thought, 'I love that man.' Instantly, you looked at the early morning sun peeping through the spring trees, and thought, 'This is such a beautiful world.' 'Then their eyes were opened.' Here you are, in this story.

And finally, on the way to Jerusalem with the news, they said to one another, 'Were not our hearts burning within us.' When does fire figure most in the Bible? When God meets Moses in the burning bush. That's the start of liberation, the beginning of covenant, the central moment of God's walk with Israel. God says to Moses, 'I will be with you.' And here, on the first Easter Day, it's the start of liberation, the renewal of covenant, the central moment in history. The disciples say to one another, 'God was with us.' Don't you feel your heart on fire, right this moment? Israel, Jesus, the Church – the whole Bible from Genesis to the maps – all condensed into one evening on the road and at the supper table. Can you look back on such an evening in your life when you now say, 'Did I not feel my heart on fire?' That's my prayer for this lockdown period, that in ten years' time we'll look back and say, 'That was the crucible of everything that followed. We renewed ourselves, reinvented church, rediscovered Jesus. 'Were not our hearts burning within us?' Here we are, in this story.

We've heard a lot about essential journeys in lockdown season. We've debated whether driving to wish your parents happy birthday is an essential journey or not. Well, this is the essential journey. This is the journey on which God's essence embraces our existence, on which our small and partial and incomplete story is fulfilled by God's wondrous and merciful and gracious story. Emmaus is the essential journey.

Behold what this story really is. 'They stood still, looking sad.' This is our life without God: bewildering, meaningless, hopeless. 'We had hoped.' We have a sense of God, Christ even, and yet it doesn't make sense; we feel let down, baffled. 'Was it not necessary.' We hear the story again, in a way that envelops and embraces but doesn't deny or obscure our story. We're swept up into a larger story. 'Stay with us.' We lower our defences and realize that we want to hear the whole story, to stay in this place for ever. 'Then their eyes were opened.' Suddenly we realize that this small story of this conversation, this meal, is not just our story, but the story of everything, everyone, for ever. 'Were not our hearts burning within us?' We go from this place with a mission to share this experience with everyone we meet, and to go through this process over and over again.

What I've just described is what we call the Eucharist. We begin confused and crestfallen: gathering. We share our stories, in all their fragility: confession. We hear God's story: readings and sermon. We resolve to eat together: communion. Then our eyes are opened in the breaking of the bread. And we leave realizing that our hearts have been on fire.

This is conversion. This is the Christian life. This is worship. In one hand Jesus takes our story, like one half of the bread. In the other hand Christ takes God's story, the other half of the bread. And when we meet God, Christ's scarred hands break that bread and our whole story is conjoined in the broken body of Christ. And the two stories become one story: now, and for ever.

Is anything too wonderful for the Lord?
Genesis 18.1–15, 21.1–7 (14 June 2020)

I have a friend in America who for the last few years has known he has a life-threatening condition. About six weeks ago he sent me a message to say he was now at the hospice stage and it wasn't going to be long. 'No one,' he said, 'has ever made it more than 30 days from here.' I wasn't sure what to do so I wrote him a letter. The letter recounted to him the jokes he'd told me that I'd never stopped finding funny, even though he first told them 30 years ago.

Most of the jokes aren't suitable for a sermon, but here's one, updated to 2020 circumstances. President Trump has a lot on his mind, so he starts wandering around Washington DC, going up to the landmarks of his distinguished predecessors. He goes to the Washington Monument, and asks, 'What am I going to do about the virus?' After a long silence, a voice says, 'Go to the people.' He continues to the Jefferson Memorial, and asks, 'What am I going to do about Black Lives Matter?' After an even longer silence, a voice says, 'Go to the country.' Finally President Trump goes to the Lincoln Memorial, and asks, 'What am I going to do about people saying I'm unfit for office?' Straight away Abraham Lincoln responds, 'Go to the theatre.'

That joke is an example of what we could call the humour of resistance; or, to give it a grander name, the laughter of the oppressed. It's a kind of humour that galvanizes a community to realize that, in the face of the powerful person in their lives, they have alternatives beyond responding with physical force. They have every kind of subversion, of which ridicule is one. In the old Soviet Union people used to say, 'One night a train stopped in a snowstorm. Lenin went to the cabin to re-educate the driver. The train remained unmoved. Stalin went to the front and shot the driver. Again, no change. Finally Brezhnev went through the train pulling down the curtains and telling everyone the train was moving.' It's how people cope when overthrowing a regime isn't an option.

There are, broadly, three kinds of jokes, of which the humour of resistance is one. The second kind is the laughter of endurance. The year is 2032. Son says, 'Why is my sister called Paris?' Dad replies, 'Because your mum and I conceived her in Paris.' Son says, 'Thanks for being so honest, Dad.' Dad responds, 'No problem, Lockdown.' Like the Lincoln joke, this one's funny because you have to do some of the work to complete the story yourself. But it's a different kind of humour. It's sometimes called gallows humour, because it finds solidarity in the camaraderie of adversity. The bleakest cartoon I've seen in the last few weeks depicts four skeletons merrily dancing together. The caption reads, 'What a great time to be alive! It's like the Great Plague but with wi-fi.'

That's resistance and endurance. But there is a third kind of joke that's less common, yet more glorious. It's the kind of humour that doesn't need a fall guy. It hardly needs a punchline because it comes out of a place of pure joy. It's about the reframing of events that seemed grim in the light of a greater story. 'Blessed are you who weep and mourn,' says the Beatitudes, 'for one day you will laugh.' When actors gather for a last-night party, or footballers celebrate a cup final win, they look back on what seemed like setbacks or failures and see them transformed into steps towards eventual glory. When two friends reflect on a 40-year relationship, they laugh about the time they missed each other on a station platform and got so cross they didn't talk for a week. When you're smiling the whole world smiles with you, and you see the hilarity of two birds courting or two porcupines trying to mate.

Today's first reading contains two moments of laughter. It puts together two stories: one of the three visitors to Abraham and Sarah in Genesis 18, and the other of the birth of their son Isaac in Genesis 21. The link between the stories is that the name Isaac means laughter. The power of the setting is that when the visitors arrive with their news of the coming of Isaac, Abraham and Sarah are in their old age. They're not expecting a child; they're shielding.

The story describes how one kind of laughter changes into another. In the first part of the story, the visitors tell Abraham his wife will bear a son. And Sarah laughs. It's a bitter laugh – a laugh of endurance, of self-protection, a laugh that isn't about something being funny, a chuckle that says, with painful irony, 'Don't make me laugh.' But then Sarah denies she laughed. The story explains, 'for she was afraid'. What an insight into the life of a woman in her culture: her body, her fertility discussed by men while she prepares food, and when she thinks they have said something ridiculous, she has to lie to hide her reaction. But some while later, she is transformed from the bitter, ironic laughter of endurance to the effervescent, gregarious laughter of joy. 'Now Sarah said, "God has brought laughter for me; everyone who hears will laugh with me."' She's like the two lifelong friends smiling at their early misunderstanding at the station – she's laughing at her own earlier laughter, for now the story has swept up all her sadness and failure and made everything into a pathway to joy.

The question that sums up the whole story is the one the visitors ask Abraham: 'Is anything too wonderful for the Lord?' I want to suggest to you that this question not only sums up the whole of the Abraham story; it also sums up the whole Bible, and the whole experience of faith. Let me explain.

I want to trace for you a line that connects a series of moments that together constitute the biblical story. Originally there's nothing. God speaks, and creation comes into being. Without God speaking, there would be nothing: no universe, no earth, no people, no you and me. Hold that thought. God comes to Abraham, the three figures of the Trinity visiting the tired and barren Sarah and her husband. God speaks, and life comes into her womb. Without God, there would be nothing. A millennium later, Israel is in exile in Babylon: the situation is hopeless. God says, 'Comfort ye, my people, I'm preparing in the desert a highway for you to go home.' Without God, Israel would still be in Babylon. There would be nothing. Five hundred years later, Mary's a virgin. Yet Gabriel tells her she will bear the Lord. Without God, there would be nothing. Yet Jesus is here. Thirty-three years later, Jesus lies in the tomb. It looks like the end of the story. Yet the Holy Spirit calls him out and there is resurrection. Without God, there would be nothing.

Do you get the idea? Is anything too wonderful for the Lord? The Bible is a series of stories in which things seem to be utterly hopeless, but right at the very utmost point of despair God gives birth to joy. Is anything too wonderful for the Lord? Over and over, God turns the bitter laughter of defence and endurance into the overflowing laughter of convivial joy. Every single time it comes as a surprise. But see what the Bible is: it's not a concatenation of judgements designed to make us all failures and catch us out as miserable sinners; it's a whisper, a rumour, a meme, a subversive word of resistance that gathers into a crescendo saying, 'There's a story bigger than the story you think you're in. It'll embrace you and lift you up when you are at your moment of despondent despair. It'll surprise you even if you've immersed yourself in its patterns and mysteries. However much you weep and mourn, one day you will laugh. Nothing is too wonderful for the Lord. Not back then with Abraham. Not in the story of Jesus. Not now, in the midst of the pandemic. Not ever.'

Christianity isn't a bleak form of endurance, an extended form of mordant humour designed to keep our spirits distracted in the face of grief too devastating to face. Christianity is, instead, faith in God's promises, which time and again have brought wonder out of nothing, birth out of barrenness, homecoming out of exile, hope out of despair, resurrection out of death. Sometimes when all seems lost, we laugh subversively in the face of our persecutor, resisting the circumstance that oppresses and depresses us. But that laughter is just the foretaste of a laughter that transcends it, a laughter that creates a community, as Sarah discovers when she says, 'Everyone who hears will laugh with me.' It's not merely a laughter of endurance, and it's not limited to a laugh of resistance. It seems most often to come at the end of a long period of barrenness, exile, isolation, misery, failure or abandonment. But in the end it's a laughter of never-ending joy.

At some point in our lives we each have to face a choice about which story we're living in. Well may we say, like Abraham and Sarah at the start of this story, that this story is about us: life's too hard, some things will never happen, faith is a bitter, sarcastic form of endurance that finds humour in irony and spots absurdity in pomposity. But we each have an invitation to see things like Abraham and Sarah at the end of this story: it's not a story about us; we're given the grace to play a role in a story that's fundamentally about God – a God who becomes most visible at our times of greatest despair, when we can't imagine a good outcome, but discover that nothing is too wonderful for the Lord. Then the joke is a very different one. Christians are those about whom Sarah spoke when she said, 'God has made laughter for me. Everyone who hears will laugh with me.'

Each morning for the last six weeks I've expected to wake up to news my friend in America was dead. But it hasn't come. So last week I called him. He said, 'I'm sorry, I don't seem to be dead.' And we laughed together as if he'd told one of his old jokes of yesteryear. Then he said, 'You know, there's nothing like being supposed to be dead to make you feel alive like never before.' It was the humour of resistance, and the humour of endurance. But it embraced me in something more than that. He was telling me he has accepted his invitation. He has seen that this isn't a story about him. It's a story about God. And he and I are lucky to be in it. He's Sarah. He's been caught up in such wonder and mystery that his resistance and endurance has been transformed into joy.

What Sarah discovered is what my friend has taught me: in the end, we shall all be embraced by the laughter of God.

The winter is over: Song of Songs 2.8–13 (5 July 2020)

When you wake up in the morning it can take a while to find your bearings and work out where you are, what time and day it is. Then suddenly it hits you – if you've had a bereavement or a break-up, it thuds in your head; if you're living with anxiety or fear, it trembles through you; if you have a hospital appointment or interview or difficult meeting, you shudder and take a faltering breath.

We all woke up this morning and had to find our bearings. But where are we? Are we in the middle of a nightmare, or should we be grateful it's worse for others? Are we in a swimming pool, flailing around trying to get to the handrail on the nearest side, or are we becalmed on a boat on a peaceful lake where nothing's happening and we're glad to hear the sounds the noise of life usually obscures? Are we at the start of a pandemic, near the end, or somewhere in the middle? Is being in church a sign that the plague is over, or a premature celebration when the worst is yet to come?

Today's poetry from the Song of Songs invites us to reflect on the season of winter. In many ways the pandemic resembles winter. Growth has been clawed back, life has been curtailed. Some of this has been for good, just as the wizening of winter can benefit a tree or shrub. But some of it's been devastating: wedding plans ruined, projects derailed, one-off opportunities lost for ever, work asphyxiated. Winter kills. Mercilessly. Sometimes for good. Other times cruelly. We can all think of ways our lives have been in winter, perhaps for longer than the pandemic. Perhaps always.

So hear the words of Song of Songs. 'The winter is over.' Over. Feel the wonder, and the power, of those words – especially if you've dwelt in winter for a long time, or always. If you're LGBTQ+, and you perceive you're not going to be despised or excluded any longer. It's over. If your child has had a life-threatening condition, and after 18 months of gruelling treatment the doctors give you the all-clear. It's over. If you never thought you could have a baby, and amazingly you hold a newborn in your arms. It's over. The shame, the fear, the wait. It's over.

Long ago a friend and his wife were expecting their first child. In the last scan the doctor spotted something that shouldn't be there. My friend's baby was born healthy, but cancer lurked inside his wife's body. Six weeks later she was dead. My friend had a tiny boy but no wife with whom to be a family. It was winter. Deep, deep winter, with no Christmas in the middle. Fast forward five years, five tough years of growth and struggle shrouded in doubt and sorrow, and I sat at my friend's wedding. And the preacher said these words: 'The winter is over.' That long winter of loss, grief, hardship, loneliness was past. Arise, my love. My friend had found a new beloved. When it came to the vows the priest said to the bride, 'Will you take this man to be your husband?' But then he gestured to the front row, and a five-year-old in full morning dress stepped forward. And the priest now said to the bride, 'Will you take this young man to be your son?' Turning to the child he said, 'Will you take this woman to be your mother?' The winter was over. The flowers appeared on the earth. The voice of the turtle-dove was heard in the land.

That's the agony of winter. That's the power of the word 'over'. That's the wonder of being able to say, 'The winter is over'.

Think about the significance of that phrase in the context of the whole Bible. The pivotal moment in the Old Testament is the exodus, where Israel escapes from slavery in Egypt and its oppressors are engulfed in the Red Sea. The winter is over. The most poignant part of the Old Testament is the exile, a kind of 50-year prison sentence in which Israel is transported 1,000 miles east to Babylon. There Israel spends a long winter, understanding its history, compiling its memories, reimagining its future, rediscovering God. But eventually, to everyone's surprise and delight, a new king sends Israel home. The winter is over. Then in the Gospels Jesus appears and announces the kingdom of God. The reign of sin and death is to end. We are no longer to be chained by mortality. Our relationships are no longer to be poisoned by cruelty. The winter is over. This one phrase, these four short words, encapsulates the hope of salvation, the promise of glory, the truth of God's ultimate and everlasting reign.

In C. S. Lewis' story *The Lion, the Witch and the Wardrobe*, the whole of Narnia is in the depths of winter. The land is cloaked in snow. But the power of the White Witch begins to fade, and the great lion Aslan is abroad in the land. Things quickly begin to change. We read these words. The child Edmund's 'heart 'gave a great leap ... when he realized that *the frost was over* ... And much nearer there was a drip-drip-drip from the branches of all the trees.' Lewis describes the moment of his own conversion in almost identical terms: 'I felt as if I were a man of snow at long last beginning to melt. The melting was starting in my back – drip-drip and presently trickle-trickle.' The winter was over.

Feel the power and the wonder of this transformation. Notice it's not the language of victory and defeat. Too often faith has turned to words like conquer, defeat, vanquish and destroy. This isn't about some almighty battle. That would suggest that the problem with evil is that it's too strong, and we have to make ourselves mightier to triumph over it. But evil isn't too big. It's too small. It promises but never delivers; it tempts but never follows through; it dangles but never fulfils. It dies and fades as winter gives way to spring.

And that brings us to the great question of our Christian faith. Is winter truly over? Is it really springtime? The government guidelines for the resumption of public worship in churches don't say a lot about the flowers appearing on the earth, the voice of the turtle-dove being heard in our land, the fig tree putting forth its figs, or the vines giving forth fragrance. But they are clear that the time of singing has not yet come. They don't refer to humming, tapping your foot to the beat, or pretending to conduct gorgeous recorded music: but they are adamant that the time for singing has not yet come.

So is the winter over or isn't it? That's the question for all of us today, in the midst of the pandemic. And the truth is, none of us know. A million business, academic, governmental and personal decisions rest on the question. But no one really knows, however many titles they have before their name, or responsibility they hold over millions of pounds or thousands of people. And the challenge for each of us is not to lose ourselves in the minutiae of things we can't know and still less control, but to focus our thoughts and energies on the things the pandemic can't change.

I'm guessing that for each of us there's a moment like there was for Edmund, when we sense a drip-drip-drip from the branches of the trees, when we know that, even if winter isn't yet over, its demise is sure. For some that will be getting out of the house, going back to work, returning to old routines. But I'm willing to guess that there is one person you long to see again, to hug, touch, be with in a way no screen or gadget or virtual rendezvous can substitute for. Until we get to be close to that person and relax and rejoice in their presence without feeling we're breaking some kind of guideline, we won't really be able to say that the winter is over. For a number of people, gathering in church, albeit at three arms' length – being in God's presence together, sharing communion as best we can – is such an experience. Spring may not be here, but winter is over. But for others, the damage of winter is deeply felt and will abide a long time: the lost livelihood, perilous financial position, fragile health or devastated plans will rid this moment of any real joy.

And that takes us to the heart of the Song of Songs. This is poetry about intimacy. Intimacy is about making with someone an electric connection of trust and adventure. Adventure inspires you to discover, experiment, explore; trust gives you safety, confidence and acceptance. When you're intimate with someone you feel able to tell them things. It's a risk to confide in them about your past, about the tender territory of hurt, shame, regret, sadness, grief. But those things, for good or ill, are gone. It's actually a greater form of intimacy to whisper your dreams of the future, hopes that may or may not happen, possibilities that will need courage, companions and a fair wind to come true. These are things we seldom articulate, even to ourselves. They require trust and touch and tenderness to take verbal form. The Song of Songs shares a few secrets about the past. But most of it is not yet fulfilled longings for the future.

Just for a moment, imagine that the Song of Songs isn't intimate poetry about trust and adventure that by some publishing glitch ended up in the Bible. Just imagine that it's actually a love song whispered by God to you: a love song designed to melt the winter of your fear, your hurt, your doubt. Just imagine that there's a bigger story going on right now than the pandemic: one that absorbs and goes beyond the fervour of protest, the anger at injustice and the panic of poverty. And that story is God inviting you, whispering, 'Arise, my love, my fair one. Trust me with your fears and failures. Share with me your dreams and longings. Come with me on an adventure that knows no end, a discovery that's ever new, a life that knows no limit. Enter the springtime where trust becomes faith, and adventure becomes hope, and faith and hope together become love.' Turn your head, your heart, your life to God and whisper, trustingly, touchingly, tenderly, 'The winter is over.'

Because that person whom God is longing to be intimate with, longing to see after all this time; that person about whom God feels, 'Until we can touch and embrace and be close, the winter won't truly be over'; that person with whom God is dying to share in an everlasting life of trust and adventure: that person is you.

2

Meeting God and One Another Online

SALLY HITCHINER

In 2014, back when Facebook was cool, I set up an online Christian community for young adults who identified as LGBT+. At that time some of them were in churches where there was little engagement with and even less celebration of who they are. A proportion of those were giving up on their faith and others were giving up on life altogether. Many of the young adults I met considered ending their lives because of a lack of ability to reconcile their experiences of gender and sexuality and their equally immovable identity as members of churches. There was little to lose, I thought; if I set up a confidential Facebook group for them to meet each other, maybe they could realize that they were not alone. Maybe they could work together to find some solutions. After building a small group of friends of friends, we went public. Within a week the group had grown from 40 to 60, within a fortnight it was 100, within a month it was 300. And it continued to grow.

We re-formed into smaller groups to keep the sense of community meaningful, a new group of 60–100 members each year who could journey together, through tentative trust building to anger at institutions to building something constructive together, and many of them finding their life partners or being ordained; things that would have been unimaginable without this experience of Christian community online. With over 1,000 people going through a Diverse Church community, we have yet to have a single suicide. However, in the five years I led DC, one of the key things we held to was that we were not a church. The name often confused people, but I got used to explaining that we were about the reformation of the wider Church to recognize the gift of the LGBT+ people already among their members. We chose not to have meet-ups on Sunday mornings; instead we offered people the chance to link up with others in their city and try out their churches, to support each other if they wanted to go to a conservative church or to move to a more progressive one if that was where they were being called. Some needed a break from church altogether. It was understandable, and in lots of cases seemed very healthy. Over those times people said that DC was their only church ... I'd fix my smile and withhold any contradiction. I didn't want to take away from them an idea that was clearly helping to keep them going. But deep down, I didn't believe we were that. I didn't believe an online community *could* replace a church. The hybrid seemed to work. We were the equivalent of a non-governmental organization that stood in where governments aren't able to or won't meet the needs of their people. But we were always hoping for the day we weren't needed.

My biggest problem with online community was rooted in one of my most firmly held beliefs about humanity ... and something I believe is at the heart of the Christian faith.

Bodies matter

Bodies matter. Matter matters. Faces, hands, the shape of your torso, the colours and contours of your skin, the twinkle in your eye, the way you hold your head and scrunch up your nose, the slump of your shoulder, the smell of your hair, the speed of your walking, the things you love about your body and the things you wish were different: it all matters. When you encounter someone, you can't look beyond their body to see the 'real' them. There are no disembodied human beings, even dead ones; even resurrected people have bodies in the new creation. It all has value, it all has space for celebration. There seems to be no better plan than for human beings to be embodied. The old lie that it's just your soul that will be whisked away at the end of time by God, and our bodies, and the rest of the earth for that matter, will be scrunched up and disposed of, is one of my one-line wind-ups. In my naughtier moments I have a passion for one-line wind-ups: a phrase that riles a person so much they have to interject even if they're not really involved in the conversation up until then. It's a quick, playful way to find out what people are made of, what they most care about deep down, which lie they can't live with in the world. One of mine is that the physical is the opposite of the spiritual. What rubbish! You'd think these people, the Christians who spout this stuff especially, had heard that Jesus hadn't come to us as a text message. You'd think they must have skipped the Gospels, to say nothing of the Old Testament, and gone straight to the nice neat arguments of Romans when they read their Bibles. It seems to have somehow passed them by that the second member of the Trinity still has a body. God values bodies so much that God has become embodied; God took on blood, bones, muscle, sweat, hormones. And it wasn't something that was just for a greater cause. The idea was never that now we have Jesus' ideas in words, neat text on a page, that God could get rid of all that cumbersome carbon. No! God still has a body. Bodies matter to God. Your body matters to God. The Church is made of bodies, baptized bodies. On my particularly provocative days I'd even go so far as to say that's not a bad definition of church: a community of baptized and baptizing bodies.

How could we be a church when our primary engagement was through screens? However meaningful our typed conversations in the chat box, however life-changing it was for people to see posted stories and shared wisdom, it's not church. It can't be church while we're physically distant from each other, where I can't look you directly in the eye and reach out to hold your hand.

And then there's that other type of body: Christ's body in the Eucharist, the belief that of all matter, this bread and wine matter more. I'm fairly low church in many of my convictions, but even I know there is something special in that and that it is central to any church. How is it possible to be one body of

Christ unless we all share in one bread? There has been a lot of discussion about this, and others are better placed to look into the intricacies, but let's leave it at the fact that it's a problem.

'So,' as my New Testament tutor at theological college used to say, 'you've convinced me to be a cynic, how are you going to convince me to go on with life?'

My one line of response to that, and I realize that this isn't a very convincing argument if you're outside of my head, is simply that it's not what I've experienced over the past six months. I feel like Peter having experienced that the Gentiles seem to be experiencing the Holy Spirit and scrambling to relook at my theology through that. It appears the Holy Spirit *can* bring people together with each other and with God online. I don't think I believe in online church ... but I'm starting to wonder if God does.

Let me tell you some of our experiences.

When online is all you've got

The pandemic descended quickly. One week everything was normal; we'd heard increasing reports about a flu-like virus, but life continued. The next week, things were suddenly unstable, congregation members with vulnerable bodies were avoiding going out and we were all told to wash our hands. I'd seen an occasional cathedral or college chapel streaming Evensong live to Facebook and wondered if we should consider something like this if we had members of our congregation who were having to stay away from church gatherings for a while. It was worth a go. I propped up my phone on a table and pressed the button to Go Live and streamed Morning Prayer to our very sleepy church Facebook page. We didn't advertise it or imagine anyone would notice. It was only an experiment to see if the technology would work, but when I stopped I noticed that 60 people had joined us, commenting with the responses throughout the entire service. The penny dropped. This is something people want. We experimented with fancier camera angles, sermons as part of Morning Prayer, having a soloist sing.

And then, as quickly as that first stage, another stage came: lockdown. I remember the 'batten down the hatches' feel, carrying over secret stashes of communion materials from the vestry to the vicarage in case we weren't permitted to leave the house and had to livestream from there. We heard rumours that there would be an announcement from the Prime Minister about a full-scale lockdown. My partner and I knocked on the door of Richard, one of our priest colleagues who lives in the vicarage apartments next to the church with us. 'Come for a last walk, we've heard a rumour we might not be able to go out after tonight.' Together we padded through the streets and the park at twilight, clinging to every last sight of trees and buildings and people. Thankfully, when the announcement came, it included one trip outside a day for exercise. But our physicality was still limited.

Trafalgar Square, where we live, quickly drained of people. Roads became the same as pavement. We pushed open the windows to hear … nothing. No traffic, even in the distance, no aeroplanes, no shouts, bangs, building work, nothing. We were left.

The conviction that I recall most starkly from those days is that people are carried by the regularity of simple worship. Richard had spent some time as a monk, and both of us had experienced the power of routine liturgy in sustaining and anchoring us through difficult times. We continued livestreaming Morning Prayer, and quickly gathered about 200 regulars from our congregation and beyond. Many said they never normally engaged with church but stumbled upon us and found comfort and kindness in the words of the liturgy. To my surprise, however, the internet had space for it being more than words. Because it was audio and visuals, and perhaps most importantly, because it was live, it felt human. We made mistakes and giggled them off. 'Oh sorry! That's the wrong Psalm.' We invited people to share the friends, family and situations they were praying for, and we would pray for their things as much as asking them to pray with us. I still have no idea who 'Annabel in Hong Kong' or 'Baby Theo going for an operation' are but I've prayed for them every day with our community online, so they are now etched into my heart. I've never met the people who faithfully asked us to pray for them, but I care about them as if they were long-known parishioners. Baby Theo did well in his operation, in case you were wondering; though I still don't know what it was for. The names of those who joined us became familiar, known, ours. We didn't stop turning up to pray with them and they didn't stop turning up to pray with us. I'll be grateful to them, these people whose faces I've never seen, for the rest of my life. In that community I found the steadfastness of God.

Like a lot of churches who ran daily services online, we found new friends. One person turned up at church the first week we opened the doors again. He found me after the service and greeted me like an old friend. 'I'm sorry,' he said. 'I feel I know you so well. I've been tuning in every day of lockdown.' It turned out that he had not physically been to church for a long time. But with the start of the lockdown, he'd travelled away from his friends and support to live with his elderly parents and ensure they got the care they needed. The isolation began to hit home, and as he was walking on a beach one day he said a prayer that God would send some support. That evening he stumbled across us. He started joining us online for Morning Prayer and we quickly became part of his daily routine. It was moving for both of us to hear how something as simple as saying a very basic Anglican Morning Prayer had been so fundamental to him. 'We weren't very professional,' I said. 'Oh, that was the best bit,' he said. 'It felt like you were human beings, friends. When something went wrong you just laughed it off. It helped me to do that in the rest of life.'

Bringing us together

Our congregation too found a new way to be together. In spite of my admission at the start of this chapter that in 2020 Facebook seemed to have passed its heyday, we decided to use it as our primary platform. While we used other platforms – WhatsApp for small group chat (particularly for our young adults), YouTube for some of our pre-recorded material,

Twitter and Instagram for announcements and engagement with the wider world – Facebook, for all its faults, seemed like the only space that wasn't a performance with detached praise or criticism for posts. We wanted to build a more collaborative engagement in both our worship and our community life, a space where it was possible for contributions from congregation both known and new to be incorporated quickly into conversation with us. A time of pandemic seemed to need more of a kitchen table for shared exploration rather than a platform where perfect products could be displayed. The Christian faith too seems to lend itself more to an engagement that is less detached. With a product on YouTube, participants are viewers who can give you a thumbs up or not. What we wanted was a space where we could build something together: an invitation to explore the gifts of all those in our community, not merely the small number who are employed here.

We set up a confidential congregation page and congregation members were able to take risks to offer material to each other. Our lay reader started holding weekly baking workshops and members of our choir joined other people in the congregation in leading a nightly service of Compline. Perhaps the most notable experience of lockdown was a member of our congregation who is often housebound and finds social interaction challenging deciding to post a daily Lectio Divina. One of the exploring faith courses that Sam and I led was almost entirely made up of people who were housebound and had no way to go to their local churches. While the pandemic was challenging in other ways, 'Finally!' one person exclaimed, 'The world is set up for people like us.' Here are people who were looking to explore faith but who couldn't get to churches because of physical limitation, now bringing the people they are into the body of faith.

We are about to set up a group of online stewards for our services. They do pretty much what stewards do in our offline services. They ensure that those present have access to our order of service. They welcome and answer any questions and facilitate newcomers in engaging with the service.

In our Morning Prayer it quickly became our custom to invite worshippers to share with us the names of loved ones who they are praying for, to be read out as part of our intercessions. This grew to become an invitation to share things they are thankful for. The experience is less detached, less a matter of liking or disliking our worship service but being in the middle of it, participating and helping to lead it by contributing to the prayers.

Portholes to each other's lives

One unexpected part of the pandemic is that we've seen parts of each other's lives that were previously private. We're not used to seeing each other's homes. I've heard it's quite common for celebrities to have fake homes for filming. When a TV chef walks into their kitchen and flicks on the oven, that's probably not their *actual* kitchen. There's something about the home that those who work in television want to protect more than anything else. Some actors will strip naked for roles but won't let photographs of their home make it onto the internet. *Hello!* magazine pays six-figure sums for having the privilege of seeing inside a celebrity's home and there's a huge market for photographs of famous people sitting fully clothed but on *their own* sofa. It appears in those situations that the home is a more intimate physical depiction of the self than the body.

Even for us non-celebrities the fact that we can see into each other's homes is still deeply intimate. Of course it is possible to blur or cover up your background on Zoom. Dozens of articles have been written about how to curate the ideal internet meeting backdrop with the perfect selection of books and carefully placed interesting artefacts brought back from trips around the world. But over time these things slip, and we are seeing more and more of our real homes, our real lives.

Children and pets are now introduced to work colleagues as they bound into shot unaware that this part of their home is now not 'home' but 'Mummy's work'. We get a glimpse of colleagues' partners for the first time as they walk past an open door or appear delivering a cup of tea. It becomes the stuff of legends if it's an evening meeting and a hand reaches into view on a colleague's screen with a thoughtful glass of wine or small plate of snacks. 'Whose partner is *that* considerate?' we all wonder.

You'd have to go back before the industrial revolution to find a time when work and domestic life was so blurred. And with this we have the opportunity to become more integrated as people and perhaps more integrated in our faith. Working from home has meant that our families see what we do at work all day. One parishioner commented that her husband said that he now understood why she was always tired, having overheard how aggressively her colleagues all talk to each other and seen how many meetings she has to fit into a day.

Christ predominantly met people in domestic settings

Christ was someone who blurred the boundary between formal and informal. He expanded the possibility of where God could be found. People in Jesus' day were used to getting dressed up to go to the synagogue if they wanted to meet God. Their ancestors had travelled once a year or every few years to go to Jerusalem for this. Jesus went around knocking on people's doors ... God went to their houses for meals; met their pets and children. Jesus is a domestic God.

Conversely, sin is deeply rooted in isolation and compartmentation. It's not just that shame often sets in and people cut off that part of their lives from the view of those who love them, certainly from those they respect. Of course we all need distance, some of us more than others, in order to have something to offer to those we love that is distinctly us. But sin pushes us beyond this to seek distance for the sake of the prop rather than for the sake of being ourselves and having that to offer to others. In order to keep some sense of ourselves as a good person, we compartmentalize our lives; we have some parts that we reserve for religion, that we keep clean and free of swear words and thoughts of the messiness of life. Like my Liverpudlian grandmother who in spite of having five children and a tiny four-and-a-half-roomed house still kept the parlour locked, set apart, chintzy and pristine, only to be opened when royalty (usually the priest) came for tea.

The luxury of not seeing into our neighbours' homes is relatively new, relatively middle class and relatively Western. In very few cultures in the history of the world would people have had closed windows and doors so that the street couldn't see how you lived. Perhaps this new season where we are present in each other's private lives has potential to make us more accountable to each other, more integrated in how we think about ourselves and each other.

At base level, Jesus shared people's homes, their domestic lives. He didn't seem to believe in compartmentalized people. If God is in our lives God is to be everywhere. I'm looking forward to discovering how joining church from our homes changes how we experience being a church community. Issues of class, caring responsibilities, mental health, disability and cultural differences become more apparent when we engage with each other not just through the clothes we wear and the image we put forward, scrubbed up on a Sunday morning, but more regularly in each other's homes. Just a thought – what if this wasn't just a practical decision based on the fact that Jesus wasn't always welcome in the synagogue? What if it was the plan? Jesus moved the centre of religion away from the power bases (though Jesus did also visit the temple and synagogues and Paul certainly made it a priority to start with them) towards the ordinary, towards the domestic. The early Church met in homes but faced significant challenges because they could only meet in the large houses belonging to the rich. This wasn't about *everyone's* homes. But now it is. Now church is to be found in each person's living room, kitchen and even spare bedroom (not that many of our London congregation have those). Church is now: not just about Sunday best, but about everyday life. Church is more intimate, more incarnate in each of our lives.

We experience conversations online more intimately

The flip-side of this is that people themselves carry a broader perspective of who they are into online encounters. Engaging with faith in one's own home changes the way we engage with it. We are relaxed, we are more open. We are also bolder online than we are in person. People are more likely to say what they are feeling, for better or worse, through the internet than in person. It's often described as being comparable to having a glass of wine.

One of the privileges of being a parish priest is that you routinely get to meet people in their homes. People are different in their own surroundings. I remember visiting a friend who had profound physical disabilities but she proudly showed me around all the gadgets she had so she could do almost everything I could do in my home. People are different people when they are in their own surroundings. There are exceptions, but in general people feel safer, they feel more affirmed in who they are, as they have chosen their surroundings or at least become used to themselves within them.

We began our new exploring faith group, Being With, shortly before the first lockdown. When we moved online, we discovered that people were more open, not less, in sharing deeply personal stories with the group. This has continued in the four subsequent groups I've led over Zoom. People seem more likely to tell of the things that have most shaped them, even things they have been ashamed of, if they are doing it from the comfort and familiarity of their own homes.

Faces

This doesn't mean that encountering one another online is without its challenges. In particular the narcissistic nature of many internet spaces is a challenge for the intrepid adventurer in encountering the other online.

David Ford, in his book *Self and Salvation* (Cambridge University Press, 2009), suggests that coming face to face with

God and one another is the dominant metaphor in understanding salvation. Ford writes how faces are deeply particularized; we are more characterized by our faces than by anything else. However, the challenge is that we do not own our face; in our lives outside of the internet other people see our faces more than we do. In some sense they are indeed the self that is offered continually to the other. The strange thing about faces is that, considering how much we care about them and how much we communicate through them, they are not for us. Even in the age of perfect mirrors, most of us hardly ever see our own faces. They are orientated towards others. More than once I've had chocolate sauce on my face from breakfast and got to lunchtime, following several meetings and conversations, before a kindly colleague tells me about it.

In early reports related to our constant use of Zoom, psychologists reveal that we are getting tired of it in part because we are constantly looking at our own face. This is comparable to some of the pressures of constantly visible self-projection on other social media sites. I suspect we will struggle to evolve to feel comfortable with this. Richard Carter led a retreat over lockdown and noticed the benefits of asking individuals to hide their own videos from themselves in the interactions. We need to discover forms of online engagement that don't involve looking at ourselves all the time. We need to develop ways of being online in which we can be self-forgetful and delight in the other.

Bread

People seem to be more, not less, incarnate online than in person. They are rawer, more encased in their physical world. They let in faith and friendships more when church groups are engaged with from our homes. However, this may not be the case if we simply put church services online that were designed for physical interaction. Eucharist is one area that the church has to discover afresh in this new era. Our old ways of thinking about it don't seem to fit.

In the book of Acts, Philip meets a man from Ethiopia, a Gentile, who evidently quickly understands and accepts Christianity. Philip's response is that the sacrament of baptism should not be withheld if this person has clearly found Christ as his Lord. Sacraments are an outward physical sign of an inward spiritual grace. If we discover that people are experiencing church in their homes, I'm not sure we can, on principle, refuse the sacraments to them, even if they are unable to get to our religious centres. The question needs to be how we can facilitate genuine sacraments, genuine Christian community, genuine church within a pandemic and post-pandemic age.

There can be little doubt that we are in a moment of great importance in the journey of the Church. The pandemic is catalysing decline in church attendance and a variety of other trends in society at large. When we look back on the pandemic in 20 years' time, what advice would we offer our younger selves now? Which issues would we urge ourselves not to care too much about? Which will turn out to be the really important ones from the perspective of the history books? If we listen ever so carefully, can we hear on the wind our future selves calling to us, suggesting questions we can be asking now that will have monumental importance? The first of those questions, I would suggest, is, 'How can we be a church discovering God and each other with everybody today?'

3

Rediscovering Contemplative Prayer

RICHARD CARTER

Two years before the lockdown, the Nazareth Community was formed at St Martin-in-the-Fields. Now numbering 81 members, this gathered community seeks to discover a life-giving way through the practice of silence, service, Scripture, sacrament, sharing, sabbath and staying with. *The City is my Monastery: A Contemporary Rule of Life* (Norwich: Canterbury Press, 2019) sets out the vision, story and experiences of this embryonic community in the heart of London – a complex, thriving city that never stops. It is a search for a rooted, attentive and more centred way of life. But then London did stop, and the city indeed became our monastery in a way we had never imagined or foreseen when I wrote this book, not just for me, and for our community, but for all forced into lockdown. It was in this totally unexpected way that the rule of life that we had humbly planted and nurtured would become, during this time, the tree in whose branches we and others could seek shelter. This path of life that we had chosen was rooted in contemplative prayer. It began with a deep longing for silence at the very centre of our city and the busyness of our lives: a silence in which we could grow in intimacy with God, neighbour, self and a fragile but miraculous world; a silence in which we could rediscover the treasure beyond all price, a treasure we had, in fear and the rush to survive, failed to recognize. As our community meditations were now livestreamed, I began to see the huge thirst there is within the wider community for a greater depth to our spiritual lives, and a real search for a meaning beyond the confines of what we have assumed to mean church – indeed beyond the values and lifestyles we had been living. Each Saturday morning at 8 a.m., meditations and walks and regular times of silence during the week, became a way of connecting with people across the country and indeed across the world. In this chapter, adapted from the letters I wrote to members of this community, I share the diary of some of our discoveries.

Why contemplate?

I have been reading some of the writing of Evagrius Ponticus. He was a fourth-century Desert Father who spent a lot of time in prayer, and became the teacher of John Cassian, another great writer on prayer and the Christian spiritual life. I would like to share two of his thoughts:

1. We need to rediscover space and silence in our lives in order to come home to God and home to one another. Coming home means rediscovering an intimacy with God, with our own true selves, with our neighbour and with the world.
2. The incessant conversation in our minds, the chatter, can tempt us away from God and indeed from truth. What we seek is the stillness beneath the chatter, like the depths beneath the surface waves. God's silence is actually much deeper and more truthful than words.[1]

We are always moving so we don't always see, always talking so we don't hear, or we hear in snatches, or bites, but are not able to listen to the heights or depths.[2] We hear only the notes and the discords, but not the music, or the silence in which the music floats. You actually have to stop to see and to be still to notice. Have you ever found yourself needing to do so many things at once that you end up doing nothing? Have you ever tried to eat everything so quickly you have actually tasted nothing? How often we walk through rather than staying with,

---

1 See Martin Laird, *An Ocean of Light: Contemplation, Transformation and Liberation* (Oxford: Oxford University Press, 2018), pp. 78–86.

2 Richard Carter, *The City is my Monastery: A Contemporary Rule of Life* (London: Canterbury Press, 2019), p. 8.

walk past without offering time or space. We rush to take the photo without realizing that the true camera is our inner eye. We think we have to catch up with the world. Actually we have to be still enough to let the world catch up and meet with us in the still place.[3] Christ calls his disciples to stay awake with him. That call is a call into intimacy.

Thomas Merton, in *New Seeds of Contemplation*, writes that contemplation is not a painkiller, for it will involve the anguish of knowing that God is not a graspable thing, or a miraculous answer. Rather contemplation is a seed of new life, a dialogue of love, an intimate encounter with that which we do not own or possess. God is seeking our awakening. Opening to us a new being, a new reality. It is 'sowing in ourselves the seeds of his life'.[4]

We often think of these revelatory experiences as heightened moments of transfiguration. But perhaps the real transformation begins not in the escape from the moment but when we face the present, because there is no other way forward. The pandemic is teaching us not to look without for answers but to look within. Abba Moses, one of the great Desert Fathers, would counsel his monks: 'Go, sit in your cell, and your cell will teach you everything.' During lockdown, many of us have been confined to our cells or home or 'bubbles', and realized it is not always easy. I remember the advice that if you think someone is a saint, first go and ask his or her family at home and they will soon tell you the true story. Nelson Mandela, in a letter to Winnie Mandela while he was in prison, wrote:

> ... the cell is an ideal place to learn to know yourself, to search realistically and regularly the process of your own mind and feelings. In judging our progress as individuals we tend to concentrate on external factors such as one's social position, influence and popularity, wealth and standard of education ... But internal factors may be even more crucial in assessing one's development as a human being. Honesty,

---

3 Carter, *The City is my Monastery*, p. 9.
4 Thomas Merton, *New Seeds of Contemplation* (New Directions Books, New York, 1972), chs 2–3.

sincerity, simplicity, humility, pure generosity, absence of vanity, readiness to serve others – qualities which are within easy reach of every soul – are the foundation of one's spiritual life. Development in matters of this nature is inconceivable without serious introspection, without knowing yourself, your weaknesses and mistakes ... Regular meditation, say about 15 minutes a day before you turn in, can be very fruitful in this regard. Never forget that a saint is a sinner who keeps on trying.[5]

God made us, God loves us, God sustains us (18 March 2020)

Never before has London been so strangely and eerily quiet midweek in March. There is suffering, deep concern and uncertainty. The death toll from this frightening virus is mounting. I think of Julian of Norwich, living through the fears of the Black Death and holding onto three truths revealed at that time to her: God made us; God loves us; God sustains us.[6]

I wonder if in the pain and uncertainty of our time we can seek the one who is at the centre of all things. The one who made us, loves us, sustains us. I wonder if in our lockdown we can find:

- A greater stillness
- The song of the birds
- A new attentiveness to neighbourhood
- A compassion for those in need
- A greater generosity of heart
- A greater simplicity in the way we live and the things we depend upon – is there life beyond searching for toilet paper?
- The importance of the space and place in which we live.

---

5 Nelson Mandela, letter to Winnie Mandela, written on Robben Island, 1 February 1975. From *Nelson Mandela by Himself* (Johannesburg: Macmillan, 2011), p. 164.

6 Julian of Norwich, *Revelations of Divine Love* (Penguin Classics, 1966), p. 68.

When the Desert Fathers and Mothers taught the novice to 'learn to love their cell' for 'your cell will teach you everything', they were guiding them to be at peace even within the confines of their own dwelling place. For us now our contemplative prayer must seek to discover the freedom of God in the midst of lockdown. Fear diminishes, fear is a contraction. We not only lock down, we lock out. We shut others out. Of course there are very real fears, especially for those most at risk and for those we love who are at risk. This is a recognition of our own vulnerability and mortality. But our prayer also calls us to courage. Think of the image of the storm clouds that come and go – the temptation is to see our lives as those dark clouds that engulf us and to identify our own lives with them and not to see beyond the darkness. But we are not the clouds. We are the sky. The clouds come, the clouds cover us, the clouds depart. But we do not to stay inside them. We need the courage to stay, allowing the storm to pass. Christ within us is our height, our breadth, our depth: the very ground of our being.

I encourage you all in our practice of reading the Gospel for the day and reflecting upon the words that speak to you. You will find at this time that the Scriptures take on a whole new meaning. Faith comes alive when things are really at stake in our lives.

Death and resurrection (18 April 2020)

I've been imagining what the disciples must feel after the days they have just been through. Both crucifixion and resurrection. The thing is, resurrection does not mean back to business as usual. Everything has been unalterably changed. They have seen both hell and heaven. They have seen fear and death and then, in the pit of their loss, a hope they never believed possible and revelation into the life of eternity. I believe we are experiencing something of the same. There is no going back – what we are going through will transform the way we see the world. The suffering throughout the world is enormous. And yet when life itself is at stake and we are forced to see beyond – then a new heaven and a new earth begin to open up.

It can at times feel as though we are seeing the world through clean glasses that were so smeared before we could not see: and now everything has been brought into focus. Mel wrote this morning on our Nazareth WhatsApp page: 'Somehow the green is greener, the blue is bluer, the sounds are more intense, the fragrance more perfumed, but maybe this is how it always is ... maybe in deprivation sensory responses are sharpened', or maybe at such times we are given, as Bev said, 'new windows into the soul'. We are stripped of so many of the things we thought we could not live without and here, raw, real, now, we find the gardener who speaks our name. When our name is spoken, even wounds can become signs of resurrection. The secret is to see even the difficulty and our own struggle and weakness, not as the end of our path but as something 'entrusted to us'.[7] St Augustine, who certainly went through his own struggles, 'is convinced that there is nothing, no matter how defeating, that is beyond God's ability to use for our good,'[8] writes Martin Laird, and that 'All wounds flower ... The flower of the wound is the flower of awareness that is our grounding essence.'[9]

- I wonder what it is you fear.
- I wonder what you have learnt.
- I wonder if there can be a blessing in this tragedy.

I wonder what God is saying to us at this time.

Living the beatitudes (16 May 2020)

Our contemporary rule of life is something that we did not create for its own sake. It is a practice that holds us fast even when we face the fear of all that is unknown, indeed face our

---

7 Laird, *An Ocean of Light*, p. 205.
8 Laird, *An Ocean of Light*, p. 210.
9 Laird, *An Ocean of Light*, p. 217.

own doubts. We are learning to live the beatitudes. We are learning to live with an attentiveness to God both on the top of the mountain but also in the valley of the shadow of death where we need fear no evil. Our rule of life was always meant to be life-giving and that is never truer than now.

The author of *The Cloud of Unknowing* invites us 'to look over the shoulder of our distraction'.[10] This implies not that we get rid of our fears and troubles, or manage to push them away, but that we discover the inner stillness where we see beyond those fears. When we meet those fears with stillness rather than commentary we begin to realize that the trouble has shoulders – it allows us to see beyond it. The struggle becomes the means to seeing into a greater truth. This time, even when it may feel like a disintegration, can become the place of our becoming. In the cloud of unknowing we meet the one who is both beyond and intimately present.

Let's think of another image: in prayer it is often thought that we are asking God for help. If we imagine ourselves in the midst of a storm, and God as the rock that we need to hold onto, it's as if we are trying to haul this rock towards us or into our boat. But think of it the other way round. We are not hauling the rock to us – we are hauling ourselves towards the rock. We are pulling ourselves into God. What felt like drowning becomes the moment of rediscovering the rock. While the storm may rage around us, the rock is abiding, stronger and far more solid than the storm. Thus the disintegration is actually leading us to a greater and eternal strength.[11]

I spoke to a chaplain in a hospital who has been pastorally caring for the dying and their families. She told me of how when families could not visit she held up her iPad to those on the ward so they could whisper messages of love across the divide. We think of the dying as other people, not us, somehow removed from us. 'It's not true,' she said. 'It could be any one of us.' One of our own congregation is on a ventilator. I phone

---

10 *The Cloud of Unknowing*, Chapter 7, in *The Cloud of Unknowing and Other Works* (London: Penguin, 2001), p. 29.

11 See Martin Laird, *A Sunlit Absence: Silence, Awareness and Contemplation* (Oxford: Oxford University Press, 2011), p. 156.

the hospital but no one answers. I am ashamed to disturb and yet I think if it were me dying alone … I phone again. A nurse answers and tells me that the patient cannot speak but she will hold the phone against her ear. And into her ear I whisper, 'Dear N, God is with you. Nothing, nothing can separate you from the love of God.'

I dream that I am drowning, and every time I come up to the surface of the water to try and take a breath I am being pushed back under. And then under the water, in the stillness beneath the pounding of the waves above, I see Christ swimming towards me. And he breathes the breath of life into me and says: 'You can breathe under water.' And with his breath, I realize I can.

Many years ago, at the beginning of a 40-day silent retreat I was about to begin, I was anxious what I would do and how I would survive the silence without sinking into despair. I remember going to look for the gardener in the grounds, and asking, 'I wonder if during these next 40 days I can help in the garden.' The gardener answered, 'I think the real question is can the garden help you?' I wonder what it is that can help you now. For me at the moment it seems to be three things: friendship, the London parks and prayer.

In-between times (13 June 2020)

I am more aware than ever that we are living in in-between times. The difficulty of in-between times is everyone wants either to return to what things were like before or to know what the future is going to be like. Now is the time when the strategic planners are making plans that seem to unravel as fast as they plan them. But it's hard to simply live that maxim of childhood 'wait and see'.

But perhaps that is what we do have to do in the in-between time – to wait and see. This is the place not of solutions or outcomes, but of faith. Not of holding onto the past or grasping towards a future, but of living with the present. But even as I write this I know the struggle. I know too that every new beginning begins with a dissolving, every new journey begins with a parting, and the new life of a tree begins with a seed falling on the ground and dying.

It is here and now that our promise of 'staying with' becomes so important. The need to keep on turning up for God, holding the pattern we have learnt, living the rhythm of our contemporary rule of life, so that it becomes in us an internal compass that keeps on returning us to God like a magnetic north. A prayer phrase I recommend to you is this: 'Jesus has gone ahead of you.' This does not mean he has left you, but that he has prepared the way for us. Even in the in-between there is an already, and a not yet, and a presence now. The Benedictines take a vow of stability. I wonder if we too can discover that stability even in the storm. The importance of staying with is not how we bring about solutions but how we live with people, events and difficulties that won't go away. I'm always going to be faced with that which I cannot control – how do I even then live beyond resentment, murmuring, anxiety, pain without being defined by it? How can I be fully alive even in the midst of trial? I wonder if we can drink the cup of suffering and not be poisoned by it, but rather let it become for us the cup of salvation.

Hold fast by letting go
The less longing, the more presence.
The less we bang on the door, the more it opens for us
The less we demand, the more we see the beauty of the gift
The less we expect, the more the joy of the surprise
The more selfless, the more self
Clamorous need shuts us off from the needed
'It is our clinging that is our death'
The less we cling, the more we embrace,
The less we fear, the more we love
All joy reminds us
It is not a possession but leads us onwards
Our love is a taste of things to come
Go lightly
Go simply

Feel the beauty of balance
A breathing out
A breathing in
A shared breath
A letting go so that we may be held forever.[12]

Perhaps the earth can teach us (11 July 2020)

Perhaps a huge silence might interrupt this sadness
of never understanding ourselves[13]

Perhaps this stopping can change us and this pause can make us think again about the way we treat one another and the earth. Perhaps this is also a time of rebirth. There are a startling number of people who think that the contemplative life means being cut off from and unconcerned with the world and its needs. Contemplation is not passivity. It is seeking to live the risen life. But in order to live that life, we need a discipline. We often fear disciplines, because we think we will fail or, even worse, be judged for failing; though usually it is ourselves that do the judging. But a spiritual obedience is in fact a deeper listening; and it leads to a greater freedom. Martin Laird has written with such clarity on this subject, and has been a wise spiritual guide. I encourage you to read his books. Here are some insights from his *An Ocean of Light* that can help us develop our own contemplative practice.

Contemplative practice allows for more space to be freed up as our mental clutter is cleared away. God is always there. What contemplative practice does is to get through the clouds that have obscured God's presence and enter the luminous vastness beyond. We discover what it means not to be silent but to be silence.[14] We begin to discover the eternal now.

---

12 Carter, *The City is My Monastery*, pp. 234–5.
13 Pablo Neruda, from 'Keeping Quiet', trans. Alastair Reid, *Extravagaria*, bilingual edition (New York: Noonday Press, 2001), p. 26.
14 See Laird, *An Ocean of Light*, p. 108 and all of chapters 4–5.

Reactive mind[15] clings to what it wants and discards what it does not want. Reactive mind looks around at others and decides that, however they are, we must be better. Reactive mind draws its life from two things: comparing itself with others and being the centre of attention. It derives its sense of who it is from what it thinks others think of it. It is bent over itself. Its response to others is defensive, suspicious or hostile. Reactive mind allows suspicion and fear to grow, because the other is always a potential competitor or threat. Reactive mind grasps after ownership, control, territory but not depth, communion, grace. When we are reactive, our humanity is diminished. Notice the way that fear can make us reactive. Fear of criticism, or failing, or being rejected, or of not being adequate. It is an inner paranoia that sees others as threat. It is the fear of having our security taken away, or our inadequacy exposed. It is the fear of dying alone.

Receptive mind.[16] Nothing has been added to reactive mind: it is simply that more mental clutter and fear has been cleared. Reactive mind differs from receptive mind in the same way that hard dry soil differs from soft, well-worked soil that is rich in organic material. The sheer generosity of receptive mind continues its expanse, an expanse generous enough to cradle in its arms the joys and burdens of a lifetime. Pain still hurts, joy still gladdens, despair still flattens, but we are less demanding that the present moment – whether pain, boredom or bliss – be other than it happens to be. The receptive mind no longer sees one's past as judgement or shame, but as the way of becoming who we are now; and it no longer sees the future as threat, but as the possibility of growing in love.

Vigilant awareness.[17] We cannot stop the thought any more than we can stop a waterfall. Rather we learn to recognize the destructive thoughts and to name them, so that we begin to change our relationship with thoughts, seeing them as thoughts

---

15 Laird, *An Ocean of Light*, chapter 3.
16 Laird, *An Ocean of Light*, chapter 4.
17 Laird, *An Ocean of Light*, pp. 78–86.

rather than the reality that defines us. We turn away from the inner chatter of the reactive. We learn to get our attention out of the interior story. We begin to glimpse an inner spaciousness that is silence. And in this silence, compassion and awareness are born. We awaken to a new intimacy with the created world, a new intimacy of awareness to our neighbour, a new intimacy with God. It is common for the contemplative to feel on the edge or periphery of things. We can often feel quite the misfit. The place on the edge actually is where we discover our centre and becomes the place of truth and transformation.[18]

> Out beyond ideas of wrongdoing and right doing there is
>   a field.
> I'll meet you there.
> When the soul lies down in that grass the world is too full to
>   talk about.[19]
> (Rumi)

From alienation to the realization of presence (1 August 2020)

The rain falls equally on all things. (Zen poet)

Today I would like to consider how our contemplative prayer and action might help the movement within from alienation to presence. This needs us to discover a way of letting go of some of those things that weigh us down and finding a path that nurtures and brings growth. Different spiritual traditions offer guidance, and I have found great wisdom in the teaching and meditations of Tara Brach.[20] The method she uses is a helpful Buddhist practice that follows the acronym RAIN. In our meditation today I would like to use and adapt her valuable acronym for our practice. She calls this meditation After the

---

18 Laird, *An Ocean of Light*, pp. 128–9.
19 See Poetry to Share: https://nationalpoetryday.co.uk/poem/out-beyond-ideas/, accessed 20.2.2021.
20 Tara Brach, *Radical Compassion* (London: Penguin, 2020).

Rain – which is a beautiful image in itself.[21] After the rain is the time when the ground is soaked in life-giving water, the pavements washed with rain, the air smelling fresh and cleansed of the dust. Just for a moment imagine you are setting out into the sunshine after the rain.

After the Rain

R – Recognize

The first stage in a journey to a deeper awareness of God's presence is to recognize where we are and what we are experiencing. Recognition is observing your inner life. What is happening within now. Imagine your life with a horizontal line dividing it in two. The part of your life that is visible and revealed is above the line. Now recognize what is below the line: the large part of your life that is hidden. Recognize in your own life what is below the line. It's your inner weather. For example, I am really tired or I am experiencing anxiety, or I am thinking about something I should have done, or something I have done wrong. I am holding anger, hurt, guilt or blame within me. What do you recognize within yourself beneath your defences? It starts the minute you focus your attention on whatever thoughts, emotions, feelings or sensations are arising right here and now. Recognizing involves seeing the things within us that we may have been denying. As your attention settles and opens, you will discover that some parts of your experience are easier to connect with than others. You can awaken recognition simply by asking yourself: 'What is happening inside me right now?' Try to let go of any preconceived ideas and instead listen in a kind, receptive way to your body and heart.

---

21 'After the Rain'. See Brach, *Radical Compassion*, ch 3.

A – *Allow*

Allow is a liberating word. It is a word that means you are not under judgement or condemned for being who you are. Allowing says to you, and this is hard to assimilate – that you are loved by God no matter what. You are not under judgement, rather you are held in God's grace. All of you. Allowing means 'letting be' the thoughts, emotions, feelings or sensations you discover. You may feel a natural sense of aversion, of wishing that unpleasant feelings would go away, but as you become more willing to be present with 'what is' a different quality of attention will emerge. Allowing is intrinsic to healing. Its aim is to make peace with the wars or divisions within you. Allowing says yes. Yes, I'm struggling, or yes, I'm lonely or yes, I am in need of God's help. I let go of my defences and 'let the truth be'. And in letting be I invite Christ in too: not to point out the failure, but to allow his love to occupy the fearful derelict space. And the first stages of allowing – like the rain – may simply be to soften the soil or to wash away some of the self-accusations, or simply to refresh and rehydrate a part of you that feels forgotten. You can't do this all in one go. It may simply begin with a softening of the edges.

I – *Illuminate*

This is not an interrogation of self, as though you are on trial before a judge. Much more, the next stage in our contemplation is an illumination: allowing the light in to see what you could not see and may have feared. It is a seeing within. Allowing the light in means that sometimes we see the things that have made us stumble and fall. We also begin to see that some of these things we fear feel real but are not true. And that alongside all we fear, there is also the story of resurrection that we have failed to realize. Illuminating is like the moment when Thomas sees the wounds of Jesus and begins to realize that the very wounds that destroyed love can become the signs or place of hope and resurrection. When we illuminate what we fear we often find that the place we thought we would discover condemnation and shame is the very cellar of our soul where the hurt, but also the true treasure in our life, is illuminated. Or to consider another image, the darkness is the very place the seed begins to break open and the tender shoot grow into the light.

N – Nurture

The final stage in this contemplation is to nurture the good. It is the liberating realization of grace and goodness that cannot be overpowered. It is Christ's love for you as a whole person and the realization of his compassion at the very centre of all that you are. It is living in and allowing that goodness and compassion within you to grow. It is paying both yourself and your neighbour and the world loving attention. It is allowing yourself to let the compassion in your heart grow, rather than the condemnation. It is the gentle slow growing realization that you are defined by failure, but held in love. 'Among the fruits of our receiving grace is the expansion of our ability to receive.'[22] And grace sets you free, free also to share that same grace with the world. Nurturing is realizing your salvation and your blessing and that you have blessing to share: it is a new openness. Think of Jesus' words to Peter: 'Do you love me? ... Then feed my sheep.'

Wilderness time (12 September 2020)

I am aware of how little we know of the future, and how at this particular moment in time all our best-made plans can, so easily in rapidly changing events, come to nothing. A society that depends on planning and control is now trying to navigate the uncertainty of what will happen next. And yet we know that it is in the wilderness that real change is born. One can feel the forces of the reactive mounting, desiring to invade the vacated space and seize back control. But can we not also feel the wind of God's Spirit? We are not sure where it comes from

---

22 Laird, *An Ocean of Light*, p. 88.

or where it will take us but we know, indeed have already seen, that it can lead us into new life. We often fear that Spirit, because it challenges us to let go of our securities and follow the intuitions and truths of our faith. I believe that the renewal of our Christian faith involves just that: a deeper faith, a letting go of our belief that it all depends on us – our plans, our programmes, our events, our control and the realization of the power of what is beyond us in the midst of our lives – the one who calls us to follow. Here are some words from Rowan Williams that he shared with the bishops in Rome.

> Contemplation is very far from being just one kind of thing that Christians do: it is the key to prayer, liturgy, art and ethics, the key to the essence of a renewed humanity that is capable of seeing the world and other subjects in the world with freedom – freedom from self-oriented, acquisitive habits and the distorted understanding that comes from them. To put it boldly, contemplation is the only ultimate answer to the unreal and insane world that our financial systems and our advertising culture and our chaotic and unexamined emotions encourage us to inhabit. To learn contemplative practice is to learn what we need so as to live truthfully and honestly and lovingly. It is a deeply revolutionary matter.[23]

---

23 Rowan Williams, 'To be Fully Human is to be Recreated in the Image of Christ's Humanity' (Vatican City, 11 October 2012).

4

Facing Grief Amid a Pandemic

CATHERINE DUCE

A pandemic stirs up unprecedented levels of grief and fear in a population. People are struck by the realization that they are fragile and mortal. Some people die alone, separated from their loved ones. Others are left to grieve alone, uncomforted by traditional rituals and wakes. Those who haven't lost anyone personally encounter daily reminders of death. They grieve lost routines, jobs and freedom of movement. They fear for their own health and that of their loved ones. Such intense experiences plumb a deep reservoir of feelings within each individual.

During the pandemic, St Martin's walked alongside people experiencing intense grief; grief reawakened, anticipatory grief, and personal grief experienced by those in leadership and those in the pews. In this chapter I weave the story of the death of Lazarus in chapter 11 of John's Gospel into a reflection on our story together over this period. There have been many insights gained from living through such a multifaceted and intense exposure to grief. Ultimately, this chapter will suggest that this pandemic has been a sharp wake-up call to the Church to speak more boldly and prophetically about death; a subject on which society prefers to keep silence. Yet death is a sure reality for each one of us. It is a journey we can prepare for if we choose. The Church has a gift to share: the message that living with the end in mind can sharpen the quality of our living in the present. The greatest invitation of the pandemic has been for individuals to tend to their fears and to seize the invitation to live God's future now fearlessly, courageously and in the light of eternity.

Prior to the pandemic, clergy at St Martin's preached occasionally about death; it was also the subject of several theology groups. Clergy were aware at any one time of a handful of people grieving the loss of a loved one. Like many churches after a death, there would be a flurry of support around the time of the death itself, but as a church we were aware that more could be done to support those experiencing the longer-term effects of grief. In late 2019 discussions began about running a bereavement support group. A bereavement specialist, Kate Woodhouse, had approached the church offering to run some weekly grief support sessions. These plans were accelerated once the pandemic began.

Bereavement support group

A ten-week bereavement support group was offered to parishioners who had lost loved ones in the last five years, for whom full lockdown was likely to exacerbate feelings of loneliness and grief. This was not a group for the newly bereaved. It was a deliberate step to encourage and support those for whom physical isolation could lead to a painful resurgence of latent grief. With disrupted routines and coping mechanisms, people who were already vulnerable had more time to think about their losses.

Five participants, one of whom (me) was a clergy member, gathered weekly for an hour and a half on Zoom for a facilitated group session with Kate Woodhouse. Some had lost parents, others had lost partners, others had lost children. It was a time of storytelling and profound listening; of sharing memories and giving voice to feelings that often get buried or parked; of delighting in music, in God's creation, in art, photos and pictures that spoke to us of our loved ones. We were asked to write down our feelings of grief with our non-writing hand, to tune into our subconscious.

During the course, one participant missed a session to bury the ashes of her mother. In another session a participant showed boxes of belongings of their deceased loved: a sharing made possible by the intimacy of a Zoom chat room. We laughed together at some of the nonsensical behaviour we found ourselves engaging in as we clung onto past memories, such as keeping a loved one's toothbrush in the bathroom cabinet five years after they had died. The reflections below make clear that this group was not without its moments of chaos, and of sharing with brutal honesty the depth of darkness of grief, guilt, shame and abandonment. Yet bit by bit, we realized that others too had a reservoir of feelings inside that in the space of an hour could move from coping to anger to loss. Through skilled facilitation, the group navigated these waters. It was a pause in the week to reconnect with self, others and God.

What became clear was that as a church we can spend many hours together as a community; but rare is the environment nurtured that enables such a quality of non-judgemental listening. Seldom is time cleared to hear the small delights or creeping anxieties of each day, within a safe, honest context, in which people get to know one another's histories and habits.

Grief, Loss and Remembering workshop

After four weeks of lockdown in the UK, the strain was showing on church practitioners in positions of leadership, and on clergy generally. Anglican clergy were banned from entering their churches, at great personal cost. Other clergy were anxious about vulnerable family members, or found themselves shielding for reasons of ill health. Anxiety levels were high for church leaders, both lay and ordained, who were carrying the worries of the parish at large. There was a flurry of activity at diocesan level. For five weeks, some St Martin's clergy were placed on rotas to be on call at local London crematoria. New funeral services and guidelines were issued to accommodate 20-minute slots. Diocesan groups were set up to review memorial services and online facilities to commemorate those who had died. Where churches relied on commercial income, those in positions of leadership were also facing significant economic pressures, bringing their own grief.

In the whirlwind of collective survival activity, it was felt important to respond to the pandemic by offering a HeartEdge workshop entitled Grief, Loss and Remembering. Its purpose was to nurture a sense of self-care among those in positions of church leadership, and to name and normalize experiences of trauma.

The initial May workshop involved a clergy person sharing experiences and posing questions to other panellists, including a member of the Trauma and Congregations project, a bereavement counsellor and a psychotherapist specializing in trauma. The workshop was followed a week later by an optional pastoral follow-up for one hour, including a funeral director speaking movingly about the impact of Covid-19 on their mental health. In both workshops there was a sense that people were hanging on every word, so visceral and so intense were the experiences that people carried.

Reflections and insights

Here I draw out some reflections from both the bereavement support group and the HeartEdge workshops. Accompanying these insights are verses from John 11, the story of Lazarus. This is a rich story of interpersonal relationships gravitating around the death of a loved one. There are signs of potentially healthy and unhealthy grief at work in the reaction of the disciples; in the example of Jesus in his response to a crisis; and in the growth in self-awareness of both Martha and Mary. Jesus' friend Lazarus falls ill and his two sisters call for Jesus to visit. When Jesus finally gets to Bethany Lazarus has already died, and has been in the tomb for four days. The two sisters, Mary and Martha, and the crowd all exhibit signs of grief. This sight moves Jesus to tears. Here is a beautiful illustration of the way grief is never static, and never gets the final word. Attending to our own grief is a lifelong journey.

*Naming and normalizing death – Jesus told them plainly,
'Lazarus is dead.'*

Whenever human identity or a sense of security is threatened,
it is normal to experience an intense grief reaction. Perhaps
the central insight from both the bereavement support group
and the HeartEdge grief workshops was that *naming death*
was a key step in normalizing processes of grief. Reference to
relatives or friends 'passing away' or 'falling asleep' or 'going
to the angels' can pay a disservice to people who are grieving
or seeking to move forward after a huge loss in their lives.
The death is real and it must be named. The second discovery
is that once the death is acknowledged, then walking alongside the grieving is never about fixing their lives and making
the grief go away. It is about helping people find meaning in
their new reality. Giving voice to the deep reservoir of feelings
people experience helps to *normalize* grief, and take the sting
out of it.

There was a huge range of responses to the pandemic by
congregants and church leaders. Some well-documented reactions to trauma were evident. These are identified below:

*Initial paralysing fear, uncertainty and adjustment – The
disciples said to Jesus, 'Rabbi, the Jews were just now trying
to stone you, and are you going there again?'*

A pandemic was met initially with a chaotic period of panic,
fear and a time of frantic adjustment. Society waited eagerly
for those in authority to provide direction, and yet our leaders
often had no answers. These early experiences of the pandemic
were all voiced in our workshops. The fear of dying was acute
(dying is always a possibility, of course, but just not in people's
active consciousness), as was the jolt to people's comfortable
lifestyles. The disciples have a similar reaction to Jesus' proposal that they return to Judea to visit Lazarus. This was a
risky, life-threatening proposal. 'Rabbi, the Jews were just now
trying to stone you, are you going there again?'

Heroic phase, united together, Dunkirk spirit – Thomas, who was called the Twin, said to his fellow disciples, 'Let us also go, that we may die with him.'

Then followed the heroic phase, and this was evident early on in the crisis. The personality of individuals intensified. The active got busier and bolder. The shy retreated into places of quiet helpfulness. Those who loved to serve fed the hungry day and night. Those who could visited the shielding with food and shopping. In the first four weeks of the pandemic there was an explosion of online church and a surge of activity. The homeless were fed and housed. Bereaved people whose weekly routines had abruptly stopped took up new hobbies in the house and tended to their overgrown gardens. Zoom was an exciting new reality for those who could master it. There was great support for the NHS, with weekly clapping and neighbourly interactions. Of course not everyone felt this surge of energy; but if you were lucky enough to experience it, it didn't last for ever. Once the disciples saw that Jesus was determined to visit Lazarus, then Thomas jumped up with heroic (or naive) courage to risk his own life too. This same rush of energy is very much a feature of the newly bereaved. With the adrenaline rush of tending to all the practical aspects of a death, and with often more support from relatives and friends in the immediate aftermath, people find great resources to cope. But this can change.

Complacency and denial – The disciples said to him, 'Lord, if he has fallen asleep, he will be all right.'

After a period of time the bereaved can purposely seek ways to deny and forget the loss they have experienced. They hope it is an interlude that will soon pass away. It is too painful to acknowledge and to sit with. Philippa Smethurst articulated this very well in the Grief, Loss and Remembering workshop in her description of people's reactions to the pandemic. Some people flee the news. Other people fight it. Other people freeze. Other people faint and experience a slump in mood.

There were other hiccups nationally. The Dominic Cummings inquiry, focusing on an adviser's trip to Durham in the middle of lockdown, did great damage to a unified public spirit. As policies changed and shifted and new messaging was introduced that lacked the clarity of earlier weeks, people's complacency increased and their willingness to sacrifice freedoms for the safety of others was dented. This was not without impact for people in church leadership. The post-Easter exhaustion was not corrected by a usual week off for many, particularly clergy. When Jesus' communication of Lazarus' condition was confusing (Lazarus has 'fallen asleep') the disciples jumped on this glimmer of hope, almost as an act of denial. They sought to proclaim that all would be well and the episode would soon be over. Well, it eventually would be, but not quite in the way they had anticipated.

Disillusionment and crippling 'if onlys' – When Mary came where Jesus was and saw him, she knelt at his feet and said to him, 'Lord, if you had been here, my brother would not have died.'

There is a recognized disillusionment period after any trauma or bereavement that is signalled by an end to the heroic period. In the Grief, Loss and Remembering workshop in May, many participants signalled that they had reached this phase. There was fresh realization of the enormity of what had happened and the length of the road ahead to recovery. This phase can be characterized by depression, disillusionment and hopelessness.

This is experienced at a deeply human level. It can be frightening to experience this depth of despair and darkness. No amount of tears can clear the scene of devastation ahead, at the dawning realization that your loved one will never return. Both Martha and Mary cry out, 'Lord, if you had been here, my brother would not have died.' If only. In these moments we replay again and again the scenarios had things been different. The different possibilities become a broken record in our mind. The crowd at another point in the story cries out, 'Could not he who opened the eyes of the blind man have kept this man from

dying?' Naming the what ifs, the oh whys, the painful alternatives had this crisis not occurred is part of the healing work of
bereavement care. It's certainly what was gently teased out in
the bereavement support group, offering little transformations
at different moments to each individual, after small words of
kindness were shared.

*Lockdown phase – Martha, the sister of the dead man, said
to him, 'Lord, already there is a stench because he has been
dead four days.'*

This is the point of rock-bottom despair. Exhaustion levels are
sky high. Bodies are numb with pain as they experience grief
in its rawest form. Many people experienced this moment in
late June/July. Life will never be the same again. There is no
going back. There is no light to beckon you into the future.
All that people can see at this stage of the grief journey is the
irreplaceable absence of a central figure in their lives; a piece of
their own life and spirit has subsequently died too like a candle
flame snuffed with no lighter to burn again. Martha experienced this after Jesus requested she move the stone at the tomb
of Lazarus. All she could do was smell the visceral aroma of
death and endings. No one action or no certain amount of time
can guarantee a shift out of this darkest of phases. But shifts,
gently and gradually, do occur. Having a listening ear and a
caring community can facilitate this shift.

Moving forward – Rebuilding and living again phase

It was too early for anyone to have reached this point in a
recognized trauma cycle, but it was highlighted in the workshop. The first wave of Covid-19 was still in full swing, let
alone the onset of the second wave in the autumn. There are
hopeful signs that Mary journeyed forward to a transformed
place of grief. In John 12, Mary is at a meal table with the now
risen Lazarus. Martha is with them. Mary is making healthy
preparations for another death: this time the death of Jesus.
We read that Mary took a pound of costly perfume made of
pure nard, anointed Jesus' feet, and wiped them with her hair.

Taking steps towards 'living again' was a theme across all our work at St Martin's during this period. It is fascinating to take a look specifically at Jesus' reactions and responses in this passage from John. They mirror much of the advice shared in our workshops.

Watchful waiting – Though Jesus loved Martha and her sister and Lazarus, after having heard that Lazarus was ill, he stayed two days longer in the place where he was

Jesus did not rush to fix a situation. In a calm way he spent two days reflecting on his actions before making a move. As far as he could, he maintained his ordinary practices in a crisis. The HeartEdge grief workshop encouraged participants to befriend their grief and the grief of their congregation. They were encouraged to inhabit a position of 'watchful waiting', a phrase adopted from the NHS. They were given permission to recognize that there was no perfect way of being a church leader in this pandemic, and in fact they had within them the resources they needed to get through it.

Reconnecting people to their own inner resources – When Jesus asked Martha to recall who he was, she responded, 'Lord, I believe that you are the Messiah, the Son of God, the one coming into the world.'

In trauma people are disconnected from their resources. The bereavement support group and the Grief, Loss and Remembering workshops sought to reconnect people to their natural resources – to reorientate them. The aim was to reassure people that they had within them the resources they needed to survive this experience. Jesus asks Martha to recall who he was; in other words, to revisit established spiritual practices and human resources at a time of crisis to anchor herself. We each have deep wells of resources within us that can be redirected towards self-care. For example, in the bereavement support group we were asked to recall which activities gave us joy and reminded us of our loved ones. This question prompted me to get out the cello again, as I remembered the joy of playing the cello with my mother. I was prompted to consider which other gifts I had neglected of late, to the detriment of my own self-care. Technology enabled this sharing and discovery of buried resources. Zoom reduced the pain of isolation. People could name and identify their feelings, however bleak, which were all building blocks towards transformation. Although physically isolated, we were not alone in this collective trauma.

Living honestly with private grief – When Jesus saw her weeping, and the Jews who came with her also weeping, he was greatly disturbed in spirit and deeply moved.

Jesus was unafraid to show his grief. It was a natural part of events. Being attentive to personal boundaries was emphasized as vital. Leaders were encouraged to make space to grieve personally. This could then free them up to a public ministry of offering a curious, open, caring presence in the parish, keeping calm and communicating as clearly as possible. Only if space was made for self-care could a sustainable pattern of listening to other people be established to help people find their own way forward. The workshop also emphasized that the post-traumatic journey could take years. So where is the hope in all this?

Jesus cried with a loud voice, 'Lazarus, come out!' The dead man came out, his hands and feet bound with strips of cloth, and his face wrapped in a cloth. Jesus said to them, 'Unbind him, and let him go.'

The ten-week group was a journey of transformation and hope. We began guarded and cautious. It had its messy, fearful and chaotic moments. Each of us in our own tombs. Yet bit by bit, as we encountered one another week after week, the trust and bonds of the group formed, individuals began to take risks and we allowed a window to be opened into our internal world. The darkness was lessened by the gentle support and encouragement we each shared. As we travelled together, light began to shine in the dark recesses. Buried feelings, memories and thoughts surfaced. The group was not overwhelmed by the intensity of the feelings but members were able to sit, hold and be curious with each other about how they were feeling. We were offered a different narrative for our grief, and this helped us find meaning in the death of those we loved. It helped us rise again. This was a narrative of love and loneliness. How we try to defend ourselves from what at times can be overwhelming feelings of grief, where loneliness, fear and bewilderment darken our lives, where we try to hold onto the person who has died, fearful we will forget them and in turn be forgotten and not loved.

Jesus said to her, 'I am the resurrection and the life. Those who believe in me, even though they die, will live, and everyone who lives and believes in me will never die.'

Ultimately, unlike much of society, the Church is not afraid of the depths of isolation experienced by a grieving person or the depths of isolation we all fear experiencing at the point of death. Being with people as they come to terms with their suffering, or as they make sense of their prognosis, is what the Church is for. Such learning is a mystery. It can be glimpsed only in part. It can involve tiny steps forward and then a retreat. But this hope the Church can speak of is called resurrection. Jesus spoke the words, 'I am the resurrection and the life'. What does Christ mean by these words? This is not a glib platitude. It is a truth that should be at the forefront of our preaching, teaching, presence and engagement. Living with the end in mind sharpens living in the present. The greatest opportunity of recent months has been for individuals to seize the invitation to live God's future now fearlessly and courageously, and to live in the light of eternity. If that can be achieved, it brings freedom to the bereaved. Death cafés, death doulas and many other initiatives exist to help people in churches speak about death. At St Martin's, we have witnessed that telling stories can unbind people and set them free both to see again the whole of the person they grieve – warts and all – and to set the grieving person free to live the gospel. Our stories find a home in a greater cosmic story of an incarnational God who is the resurrection and the life, in whom we find our hope. Here are the words of a participant in the bereavement support group:

> I feel as if I have found a new little family, and one with whom I can easily relate. I will go on to look at more pictures, listen to music, enjoy the birds singing and spend some quiet time with Jesus. I have always found him to be the way forward, the true answer to my every need and the one who brings life to me in my moments of solitude.

Further reading

Mannix, Kathryn, *With the End in Mind: Dying, Death, and Wisdom in an Age of Denial*, London: HarperCollins, 2017.

Smethurst, Philippa, *Mental and Physical Health in a Time of Covid-19*, unpublished paper, 2020.

Institute for Collective Trauma and Growth, www.ictg.org/phases-of-disaster-response.html, accessed 30.11.2020.

Tragedy and Congregations Project Resources, https://tragedyandcongregations.org.uk/, accessed 30.11.2020.

5

When I was Hungry, You Fed Me

RICHARD CARTER

I arrived at Glasgow station and asked the taxi driver to drop me at Barrowfield estate. 'You don't need a taxi,' he said to me, 'you need a tank.' It was 1986, and this was a place where nothing would grow. The blocks of flats looked like a war zone, and the only place to park a car was the police compound – or it wouldn't be there in the morning, or not much of it. The stairwells smelt of cannabis and chips; the windows were boarded up. But there in an upper window, a candle flickered, lighting an icon of Mary: and there in this upper room, behind a simple altar, the Eucharist was exposed to the poverty of this place.

I arrived in this no man's land adrift and lost, feeling I could not fall any further. I was suffering from a depression I'd been fighting for months. And here was the place of healing. I was like a man on a trapeze who has lost his hold. But instead of hitting hard ground, I found myself suspended in a safety net. It was here in this derelict estate that I found Christ. I was not offered a miraculous solution. I simply was welcomed and stayed until it was time to move on. And when I left I took this dwelling with me.

The Franciscan Brothers (SSF) who rented this house were broken into three times in the first year. That was before those on the estate recognized they were the real thing. Neighbours from the estate started to visit, to share their needs and struggles or because they knew this was a safe place to be. These brothers had not come to tell them what to do. They simply came and stayed and did not run away. Even now, nearly 35 years later, I can return in my memory to this place of healing, and in my own derelict places of fear and dread, there behind the broken glass of the break-in, I can see a candle burning, a luminous darkness and a manger of hope. Here in the place of my desolation I discovered a treasure beyond, and beyond all price. God had planted a seed in the land where nothing else would grow, entirely vulnerable, entirely inadequate, yet alive and growing within, the shoot that would become the tree in which many could find shelter. I remember the Eucharist on the altar, nothing but everything.

In March 2020 when lockdown took place I remembered that upper room as I, from my first-floor window, looked out over Trafalgar Square. The gates of St Martin-in-the-Fields, the church with the ever open door, were shut because of the virus. How quickly the steps of our church had a derelict feel – littered with cups, broken bottles and discarded takeaways that even the pigeons had abandoned. The government's advice was being constantly repeated – stay safe, sanitize your hands, socially distance, work from home. But what if you've got no home, no place to sanitize or socially distance? Westminster Council, working with the homelessness agencies, had done well getting many into hotels, but now everywhere was shut – the day centres, the libraries, the bus station, the toilets, the museums, the night shelters; even Heathrow Terminal Five was closed at night. Those who live hidden lives of destitution, or on zero-hour contracts with *zero* hours, gathered in Trafalgar Square, waiting in hope for street food handouts and hotel places that never came.

It's painful to see raw need. You want to turn away, not because you don't care, but because you care too much. The desperateness seeps into you. You feel the guilt and frustration of powerlessness building within like a pressure cooker with no way out. Ian, the elderly gentleman sitting outside for the last two weeks, is still looking for cigarette ends to smoke even though he knows how dangerous it is. One contaminated butt and he too will have the virus. Fiona from upstairs and I feed him cups of tea and sandwiches. Every day I phone up the council for him. Every day he waits for hours in the sun. I feel the intensity of it. The guilt and the pain lie in having no answer. It's here that prayer begins: his becoming mine.

What should I do? And the only answer is, 'Stay.' Stay like those brothers in Barrowfield stayed. So often we long to be the solution, the answer, to be the saviour ourselves instead of recognizing that the saviour is staying with each one of us. We are the Church. There on the steps, amid the litter and the smell of desperation. Each one of us seeking the home we long for. Remember the story of St Martin? It's not the compassionate St Martin who is Christ, it's the beggar. 'It's not your fault,' my godmother says to me on the phone as I stand looking out of the window feeling the pain in my guts as I see all those waiting around my door. 'What do you mean?' I ask. 'Covid-19 is not your fault,' she says. There's a lesson in this. There's a lesson in the stress we're all feeling. Somehow the 'me' must become 'us'. You can't sort other people's lives; but neither can you turn away.

Our own work with refugees facing destitution and those with no recourse to public funds could no longer be done indoors for fear of spreading the virus. So we begin meeting on our doorstep instead – 40, but then others join them, 60. Then 100. Then 160 people lining up, waiting patiently for food. We attempt to feed everyone who comes. At all times we try to preserve the two metres social distancing, round the block, and we give out masks. There isn't enough food for them. But then the local Punjab restaurant offers help – a weekly curry for 60. No payment; Amrit, the manager, simply asks that I say a prayer of blessing for his family and staff. I stand there praying through my mask for Amrit and his family, who are Sikhs, and for Joaquim Menino Fernandes who works for him and is a Catholic from Goa and whose wife in Goa has just had a baby girl. And then a group of St Martin's volunteers originating from the UK, Nigeria, Ghana, Nepal, Norway, Philippines and Botswana join me in handing out simple takeaways in a bag. Eucharist – hot chicken or vegetarian curry and rice, hand sanitizer, a clean mask and water, a cereal bar and a piece of fruit.

Some of those who are homeless are vulnerable and are known so well to us, but all the council places are full. We manage to find another hotel ourselves with individual kitchens and bathrooms. We don't know how we can afford it, but miraculously donations arrive from members of our congregation and beyond.

'Do you have an exit strategy?'

'No.'

'What will happen in three months? Where will they go then?'

'I don't know.'

All I know is that when your family has a problem you have to stay even without answers, do what you can. 'Don't think how you can transform the lives of the masses,' Mother Teresa used to say, 'just think how you can help today the person in front of you.' When did I see you hungry? Now. Don't ask if an act of kindness can change the world. It's the only thing that ever has.

Jesus does not ask us to end world poverty. He does not ask us to answer the problems of the virus single-handed or to have the strategic plan to safeguard the future. What he does call for is something much simpler, more immediate and more direct. 'When I was hungry you gave me something to eat,' or 'Whoever gives a glass of cold water to one of the vulnerable or rejected will be blessed.'

'A glass of cold water – how is that going to transform anything?' you may well ask. Don't we need global solutions to the violence of poverty? Of course, but often so much of our social action begins at a level that never roots itself in real lives. It becomes a strategy, a talking shop, a mission plan, or a form of trying to assume control in a way that is simply not present. Or alternatively we join a demonstration walking round the block with placards handed out by the organizers and then come home and while eating supper we see that global poverty hasn't even made it to the evening news. Our greatest strength as church is that we belong to the community, we dwell in it. We can't go home – because this is our home. Global poverty is actually sleeping on my doorstep tonight or lining up in the rain for a food handout that doesn't arrive. Jesus suggests that the kingdom of God begins from the bottom up. When I was hungry you fed me. When I was thirsty you gave me something to drink. That means now.

In the heat of late spring and summer, people are dehydrating. They can't even buy water because the shops are only accepting payment cards. I give a bottle of water to a man on my doorstep. Then, from my window, I watch how, unasked, he takes a black plastic sack and clears from the steps and street and doorstep all the discarded rubbish. I rush downstairs with sanitizing gel and plastic gloves. He smiles, surprised that someone should care about his hands – just as I am surprised that he should care about the rubbish on my doorstep. Then, as I turn to go back into my house, a homeless woman calls out with no sarcasm at all, 'Stay safe, Father.'

Abraham was homeless, and when I first met him he was completely blind. He used to come to The Connection at St Martin's Day Centre and stay in its emergency night shelter. Each week Abraham came to a group I ran called Spiritual Space. One week we listened to a recording of Louis Armstrong singing 'Wonderful World'. I asked the group, 'Do you think it is a wonderful world?' When we came to Abraham's turn to answer, he said: 'Yes, because now I can see.' For several years, cataracts had blocked out his vision. During our dramatized Passion Play in 2019 he played a disciple, and used a white stick, and had to be led by the hand by Ozzie to the Last Supper and then into Gethsemane to watch and pray. It was a moment that expressed so powerfully the nature of Christ's inclusive call and the community of Christ's disciples. He then had two cataract operations and, miraculously for him and for us, could see again with both eyes. And it was as though his whole body had become filled with light. So I asked Abraham: 'Do you think it is a wonderful world because you can see or did you still think it was a wonderful world when you could not see?' Abraham thought for a moment and then answered, 'When I could not see I still thought it was a wonderful world because I could see with my heart.'

'What could you see with your heart?' I asked.

'Kindness,' he answered. I remembered these words. Remembered them when out of the blue, Abraham, who was still homeless, was arrested and locked up in the Immigration Detention Centre at Gatwick. We visited him three or four times a week, tried desperately to get him released and to find legal support, and agonized when we heard that he was no longer there. They came for him early in the morning – five Home Office officials to remove this gentle man with no opportunity to tell anyone. It was only later that we heard that he had been deported. He texted me and I phoned him. 'I can hear cockerels crowing,' I said. 'Yes, this is Africa,' Abraham said. He keeps in touch. He said that he felt like someone on a ship crossing an ocean who has been thrown overboard in the middle of the sea so that he no longer knew in which direction to swim but is simply 'in the middle of nowhere'. He writes: 'This is the story of someone who has spent a decade in a place trying to build a new life only to be torn away and returned to face the violence and poverty you have fled.' But in another of his messages he writes this:

> Today is Wednesday, and the time for the St Martin's service of Bread for the World. I remember how I used to wait for Wednesdays like children wait for Christmas. The service was so helpful and encouraging to me. It fed me. I just want you to know I may be thousands of miles away but my heart is still with you all. I miss you, I miss St Martin-in-the-Fields, and I miss everyone. I am eternally grateful to St Martin's – you guys welcomed me with open heart. Though I was a slave, you treated me like a king ... Thank you for being a family to me, thank you for listening to me and showing interest in my life. Thank you all for being there at the drop of a text ... My light in the darkness. My shelter in the storm.

I quote these words because they show, I think, that even when we cannot provide the outcomes we hope for, even when we fail, the being with lives on. God's grace continues its work of salvation even when justice fails. We cannot take away the pain of Abraham's deportation after more than ten years in this country, but our faith reaches beyond time and space and allows us to be with him. Last week at Bread for the World, in the middle of a pandemic that has locked down both our nations, Abraham's voice was once again heard in our church.

He was leading the intercessions for us. He had sent a sound file that was now being livestreamed. A modern epistle to the Londoners. You could hear the congregation listening for each word he spoke – as precious as the words of an apostle to us – against a background of traffic and cockerels crowing in Lagos. It was Bread for the World.

Greetings from Nigeria. It is your brother in the Lord, Abraham. Almighty God, I thank you for giving St Martin's the Spirit of love to love you with all their hearts and minds and above all to love their neighbour as themselves. O Lord, continue to feed them with this Spirit of love. From you comes that love. Give us the heart to proclaim and offer this love to those who need it most. Amen.

In September we began the move back from the streets into The Connection at St Martin's Day Centre. It's hard to build relationships while just giving out food on the street. Inside The Connection there's a chance for hot showers, a hot meal and a laundry to wash clothes and to talk. We struggle with so many Covid safety requirements that I am anxious that all sense of community and welcome will be lost. But of course the most important aspect of this welcome is that this is a safe space. And so we have temperature checks for everyone, and face masks, and numerous hand-sanitizing procedures, and contact tracing, and one person per table and at least two metres between anyone, and two sittings and strict number counts. The first few weeks feel so regulated and alienating that I wonder if our guests will ever want to come again. But they do, of course. And on the third week I realize that the essential rules have become familiar, and the joy of welcoming people back is overcoming all awkwardness. The Punjab restaurant has provided a delicious chicken curry, a vegetarian curry and naan bread. Jeff has prepared a huge shepherd's pie, we have cooked 10kg of rice, and everyone has brought fruit. I watch as those who originally came to our group as homeless guests have now become the hosts. Serving their homeless brothers and sisters at individual tables, they ask, like waiters:

'And which would you like, chicken or vegetarian, or delicious shepherd's pie?' And I realize what Christ meant and what a joy and blessing it is when the last shall be first.

In his *Nazareth Manifesto*, Sam Wells writes this:

A Nazareth Manifesto: Being with God

1 Our calling is to imitate the way God is.

2 Our clue to how to imitate God is to follow the way God is with us in Christ.

3 Our first awareness is the abundance of God and our own scarcity – together with our gratitude that we have been given so many ways to transform our scarcity into God's abundance.

4 It is a miracle of grace that God meets our scarcity through the abundance we discover in those apparently more exposed to scarcity than ourselves.

5 A community seeking regeneration has already within it most of what it needs for its own transformation.

6 We do not configure situations as problems needing solutions.

7 We cannot understand, listen to, be taught by, or receive grace from people unless we inhabit their world, which we see as valuable for its own sake.

8 There is no goal beyond restored relationship: reconciliation is the gospel.

9 The centre of ministry is worship (being with God); and the centre of mission is being with the disadvantaged and receiving abundance from them.

10 Being with is both the method and goal of social engagement.[1]

And I realize this is what we are truly witnessing. In the scarcity of hunger Christ has shown us the abundance of his grace.

---

1 Samuel Wells, *A Nazareth Manifesto: Being with God* (Oxford: Blackwell, 2015), pp. 27–31.

6

Singing the Lord's Song
in a Strange Time

ANDREW EARIS AND SAMUEL WELLS

St Martin's has long been famous for its music, largely for
two reasons: the Academy of St Martin in the Fields, founded
in 1958, is the most recorded orchestra in the world; and the
church has a marvellous acoustic, so it has become a venue for
countless concerts – lunchtime series of 70 years' standing, and
since 1987 an extensive series of up to 200 evening concerts a
year. In recent years St Martin's has begun to develop its own
musical profile more intentionally, with a plethora of professional and voluntary ensembles offering worship, performance,
and hybrid events combining the two. This chapter tells how
St Martin's responded to the pandemic in its music ministry.

March to Easter

During the period between the virus arriving in the UK and the
first lockdown in March 2020, events moved very quickly. We
realized we had three considerations to ponder. First, we recognized that the key to sustaining worship and music was going
to lie in adapting to online platforms. We started to livestream
Morning Prayer each day, and included a soloist and pianist
to enrich the liturgy. This extended to Sunday worship also.
When the first lockdown began, and that was no longer possible, we were able to draw on our archive of choral music. We
were glad to find that we had a good deal of Lent and Easter
music already recorded.

Second, we had to establish to what extent we could support our musicians. Among these, we had our contracted choral scholars, part of a year-long apprenticeship programme, our St Martin's Voices, a company of freelance singers, most of them graduates of our scholarship programme, and our voluntary singers, notably the Choir of St Martin-in-the-Fields but also our Children's Voices and St Martin's Chorus. Life as a free-lance musician can be precarious at the best of times – but it was quickly apparent that opportunities were going to dry up almost entirely.

Third, through broadcasting and our HeartEdge movement, St Martin's has a long tradition of supporting the wider Church. Many local clergy and congregations found themselves bereft of ways to connect with and support their communities. Could we put all our challenges together and take initiatives that met all three considerations?

On Mothering Sunday the Archbishop of Canterbury made a broadcast to the nation on BBC Radio 4 and local radio. We pulled together a quartet on the Wednesday evening before lockdown began and recorded music to accompany the service. The service appropriately opened with Jan Struther's 'Lord of all hopefulness'. The Church of England started to produce weekly online services and we were able to provide music from our archive for each of these through to Easter.

Easter to July

It was quickly obvious that we could not support our own worship, let alone the Church of England's need for choral music during lockdown, with our archive alone. In addition we had a pressing need to support our musicians. So after Easter we trialled our first 'virtual' recordings – recordings made by singers in their own homes. We were in unknown territory. So we tested various methods. We landed on one that made the overall result very close to being an 'in-building' recording. We engaged two keyboard players who had recording facilities at home: either Graham Eccles recorded an organ track of a hymn or choral piece using a home electronic organ, or Gavin Roberts made a recording from his home piano for other genres. Then Gabriella Noble, our Choral Conducting Fellow, videoed herself conducting and singing along to the track. Next Cathy Martin, our Music Programme Manager, edited Gabriella's audio and video together with the original organ track. Cathy then sent this video out to the singers. They sang along, sending back their audio. Finally we edited the different tracks together, adding acoustic effects to make it sound like St Martin's building, to create an overall track. With this technique mastered, we brought back our Choral Scholarship programme 'virtually' – meeting each Monday on Zoom. We were pretty much the only church in the world to keep our education programme going without a break.

Our choral scholars soon embarked on a programme of recording five pieces of music each week, which was offered freely to the Church of England through its A Church Near You resource hub. The problem for local churches that were livestreaming services was that they didn't have a rights-free resource of music to draw upon; so this provided one. All that was required was a CCLI licence with a 'streaming' add-on. The results were spectacular: in the first nine months there were half a million downloads of the music.

Meanwhile singers in our professional choir, St Martin's Voices, saw their work and career development opportunities halt overnight in March. We wanted to keep supporting them. We began with ChoralCast – a daily podcast in which each of the singers took it in turns to introduce a different piece of music each day, before the whole group sang it. We created 50 podcasts this way, attracting a quarter of a million views. Our flagship Great Sacred Music programme – in which two hymns and typically six choral pieces are grouped around a theme, and spoken-word introductions and reflections on the theme are woven around them over a presentation lasting 35 minutes – could not continue in the church, so we changed the format and went online, using archive recordings. From June, we began a whole new venture, offering an introduction to the Christian faith, across four ten-programme sections: Scripture,

Faith, Life and God. Drawing on the techniques used with the Choral Scholars, we began to record new 'virtual' music, recorded in the Voices' homes; and the spoken sections were likewise recorded from home.

The result of all this activity, and reflection on the changing pattern of how people engaged with our output, led us to create a new online platform, St Martin's.Digital, operating as a St Martin-in-the-Fields iPlayer. This brought together the accumulated collection of recordings made during lockdown, together with already existing high-quality video content, such as previous years' autumn lectures from distinguished speakers, and also packages – like an Easter sermon bookended by two Easter hymns – specially made for the digital platform.

St Martin's Trust, ably assisted by St Martin's Charity, ran an extraordinary Keeping our Doors Open appeal from April to May 2020, and both the promotional material and the celebratory final event drew significantly on recordings and interviews made with and by our musicians. The campaign brought in £835,000, the large majority of which went to support homeless people in London and around the country, but some of which we retained in order, as the campaign theme suggested, to keep St Martin's doors open and our organization in existence.

July to November

Having been the last church before lockdown to broadcast choral music on the BBC, we were also the first church to broadcast as the lockdown lifted. We hosted BBC Radio 3 Choral Evensong live for four Wednesdays, beginning at the end of July. We opened, as we had previously closed, with 'Lord of all hopefulness'. In addition to our own singers, the series featured other London choirs, including the BBC Singers and the Gesualdo Six. This was an important experience for us: in addition to thawing the freeze on live performance, a moving process for so many listeners, it gave us an opportunity to establish how to record inside the church safely and in a socially distanced way. Working with the BBC production team, we carefully measured a two-metre gap, shoulder to shoulder, between each singer, in order to be fully Covid-compliant.

Emboldened by the success of our first attempt at socially distanced choral singing, we then brought our Great Sacred Music recordings back into the building, filmed for online streaming. We also began recording the weekly Church of England resource in person, again socially distanced. When it became possible for voluntary music to return in person in September, all these experiences meant that we were ready. So as not to impede the conventional shape and movement of the liturgy unduly, we restricted the Choir of St Martin-in-the-Fields to six or seven singers each Sunday, although for special occasions, like our Advent Carols, when access to the altar was not required, we managed to extend this to 14. The presence and contribution of a robed and talented choir trans-formed our Sunday worship overnight from willing and dutiful to lively and inspiring. It was a major threshold in our quest to lift the spirit of our community and restore in-person worship in as much of its glory as possible.

At this stage it was possible to begin our concert programme again, albeit in limited form. Thanks to a grant from the St Martin-in-the-Fields Trust, we created a series of three online concerts, with no live audience, filmed in St Martin's – A London Sketchbook, A Celebration of Bach and The Glories of Venice. This was a unique initiative for us: another first-time adventure. Over 1,000 people bought tickets. It was a further opportunity to bring encouragement to our audiences, provide work for our musicians, and develop a new way of working. Building on the summer programme, we were able to inaugu-rate a new twice-monthly socially distanced concert series with the Academy of St Martin in the Fields. The opening concert was the Fauré Requiem with St Martin's Voices and soloists Roderick Williams and Carolyn Sampson. A grant from the National Lottery Heritage Foundation enabled us to purchase professional-standard video-recording equipment. We were now able to move to another new project – a mixed model:

we had two 'live' socially distanced concerts on a Saturday, which were filmed and then edited for an online audience the following Thursday. During the November lockdown we were again unable to have a live audience; but we kept the concerts going online.

Reflections

The story narrated above is one of improvisation. A series of decisions needed to be made in previously unforeseen circumstances. Some worked out well, while other experiments proved unsuccessful. Some of the decisions were very painful, and, as in all parts of the St Martin's team, redundancies were unavoidable.

The Harvard leadership guru Ron Heifetz suggests that when all is well, very few decisions are really required. You can simply fall back on conventional authority structures and follow norms and procedures. It's only in a crisis that you need to make actual decisions – because a crisis, by definition, is when the usual procedures have in some sense failed. One helpful example Heifetz offers is that of the alpha gorilla, who orders the life of the other gorillas, and offers direction (to food sources), protection (from leopards) and order. When the threat presented by the leopard is replaced by the threat constituted by a machine gun, there is a crisis. The role of the leader in a crisis is to assess what is essential, what can be discarded, and where and how to innovate. In Heifetz's view every authority structure is designed to address a set of problems that were once a crisis and are now routine.

In February 2020, our music at St Martin's faced a set of challenges that had emerged over the previous few years. They were almost all good problems to have. We had a lot of people able and willing to make a high standard of voluntary music: we needed to create the right balance of liturgical and performance opportunities for them, while also making space for 'pick-up' participation of those with interest but less talent, and the nurturing of children's interest and skill.

We had a lot of interest from those making their first steps towards a career in music, and we were having a lot of success with events like Great Sacred Music that could capitalize on St Martin's other gifts that could complement our music offering: so we had to balance our professional music-making with our voluntary programme. All this activity was raising the profile of our music and diversifying the range of partners seeking to work with us: this was beginning to challenge the pattern of musical output that had been largely settled for a generation. Our close relationship with the BBC was reaching into many forms of broadcast and expression: we needed to capitalize on our growing reputation and visibility in ways that served the wider Church.

Two months later it felt like everything had changed; the whole programme was in jeopardy, nothing was certain, and our room for manoeuvre was very limited. The secret of improvisation is to fit what appears as a constricted, small story into a much larger story. In theological terms, it is to allow the Holy Spirit to fit our tiny stories into the larger story of what God is doing with the world. The story narrated above is an account of how that took place. In terms of the three considerations outlined at the start of this chapter, it's the story of how fulfilling each one of these principles enabled us to fulfil each of the others.

But that meant scrutinizing each of the principles more carefully than we had cause to do before. The first question was, 'What is music, and why is it so important for a church?' As Augustine put it, the one who sings, prays twice – in word and in song. Music transcends the words and actions of worship and displays a quality beyond either. As length, breadth and depth provide three dimensions, to which time may offer a fourth, so music adds a dimension to words and gestures. Beyond that, the making of music, perhaps particularly singing, and especially the practice of choral singing, offers an opportunity to express the deepest joys, yearnings and passions, and bring those into the company of heaven, articulating what the singers themselves think and feel, and expressing on behalf of a congregation a level of experience more profound than everyday life. Even more significant, some choral compositions have such a polyphonic construction – for example, Thomas Tallis' *Spem in alium* ('Hope in any other'), with its eight choirs, each building on one another's sound – that they come as close as any human creation to characterizing the nature of God. So to lose music, or at least live performance, as we did during the first lockdown, is not just to be deprived of a hobby or a form of expression that suits some people's taste: it is to impoverish worship, and thus inhibit humanity's encounter and discourse with God.

The second question was, 'What responsibility did we have to those who were not just committed to making such music, but had embarked on a professional career devoted to doing so?' The large majority of St Martin's staff was put on furlough in March 2020; the initial hope that we could employ most of our previous team was eventually to be thwarted by the duration of the pandemic. But the singers couldn't be furloughed, as they weren't employees: yet, with imagination, we were able to find a way for them to continue to provide online a service that we had hitherto only conceived of in the building. Perhaps the biggest achievement in this story is that we kept our young professional musicians from having to take other jobs or moving out of London, potentially ending their performing careers just as they were beginning, by supporting them through the pandemic, and ensuring that they still had careers at the end of it.

And the third question was, as often at St Martin's, 'How could we turn the situation in which we found ourselves into a blessing for the wider Church?' This required reliance on some established relationships, and the cultivation of some new ones. Because we already had a relationship with the BBC, we were asked to provide music for the key broadcast service on Mothering Sunday. Because we had a group of young, enthusiastic singers, we had the opportunity to experiment with various ways of recording from home until we landed on the best one. Because we already had a profile in the wider Church of England and, in HeartEdge, a ministry of renewal across the church, it was not so strange for us to provide music for every parish church to use, should it wish to. Because we had an experienced team of fundraisers, applying for funding from the National Lottery Heritage Fund was not a daunting exercise. We found that, free of the constraints of being a large cathedral, and with a small remaining staff team, we could be agile in our decision-making and nimble in our plans. Along the way we learned much and forged new relationships with technical experts and willing supporters. The atmosphere was one of willing experimentation on the one hand, and humble gratitude on the other. Never have the simple things seemed so precious; never have the complex things seemed so possible and necessary.

The greatest lessons are ones we already knew, but had never before discovered to such an extent. First, music is so precious to people that the loss of it is like a bereavement, and they will go to extraordinary lengths to ensure that it remains available and accessible. Second, making music is a vital form of creativity, and creativity is perhaps the single most empowering response to the despair and paralysis of the pandemic. Third, generosity is the best investment: if from the very beginning you ask, 'How can this benefit not just us but many others?' you are turning gift into blessing, and participating in the way the Holy Spirit turns church into kingdom.

7

The Virtual Gift of Art

JONATHAN EVENS

Creative contemplation

Throughout lockdown an exhibition for Lent by the artists and craftspeople of St Martin's sat gathering dust in our crypt. This exhibition, called The City is My Monastery, explored how we might deepen our lives of contemplation and action at the heart of the city. It gained prophetic dimensions when lockdown forced each of us – across the country and here within Greater London – to restrict ourselves to our cell and let our cell teach us everything. What did the artists and craftspeople of St Martin's learn in this time?

St Martin-in-the-Fields is home to several commissions and permanent installations by contemporary artists. We have also had exciting programmes of temporary exhibitions and installations, as well as a group of artists and craftspeople from the St Martin's community who show artwork and organize temporary art projects. We encourage art on three levels. One is participatory. Our artists' and craftspeople's group is what its prosaic name describes: a group for any artists or crafts-people in the St Martin's community. The group organizes a range of participatory activities and opportunities to make and create. These are open to participants of all abilities. There are periodic opportunities for participants to show their work, including a monthly drawing group, art workshops in Advent and Lent, a monthly rota for displaying work, two lectures per year with our Chinese congregations on Chinese art, and an annual group exhibition. Another level is aspirational. When commissioning new work permanently for the building, a competition has generally been held, tenders invited, donors sought, publicity encouraged, visitors attracted. A third level has been commercial. Various spaces within our crypt have been used for displays and sales of artwork – yet another host of new faces drawn in, conversations triggered, relationships made; and the church charges for hire of the space. This combination of approaches to art have made St Martin's a centre of community activity, energy and creativity.

All these events were focused on the building and all came to a halt with the first lockdown. How would those known for their creativity respond? Art critics wondered – as galleries slammed shut their doors – what the art world would be like once all this was over. However, the more immediate wondering was simply, what do we do now? In an article for Artlyst, I reminded artists of the saying from the Desert Fathers: 'Go to your cell, and your cell will teach you everything you need to know.' That is advice acknowledged by artists, for whom isolation in a studio is often essential for the creation of new work. The City is My Monastery exhibition had reminded us of the studio as cell. This enforced sabbath could be productive if used for contemplation and that was where our artists and craftspeople primarily focused their attention at this time.

Shared creative responses

Our first shared activity was to recreate our Lenten exhibition online. The City is My Monastery had been created as accompaniment to our Lent course, The Desert in the City. The Lent course explored the seven strands that form rules of life for our Nazareth Community, as described in Richard Carter's book *The City is My Monastery*. The exhibition explored themes of cities, monasteries, prayer, contemplation, community, silence, sacraments, study, sharing, service, steadfastness (staying with) and sabbath.

As the exhibition was primarily for those following our Lent course, we recreated it on the congregational Facebook page using photographs of the works in situ and sharing the texts written by the artists as exhibition labels. Online exhibitions were one of the most obvious means for artists in lockdown to display work, and the Christian community made good use of the opportunity with excellent exhibitions mounted by Chaiya Art Awards, Chaplaincy Arts Projects, Image Journal and Salisbury Cathedral, among others. Some, like our group, transferred existing exhibitions online and others created new exhibitions, often exploring lockdown themes. Some, as with our exhibition, did so using existing photographs and text; others recreated virtually the actual exhibition spaces in which the works were shown.

Our practice in Advent and Lent has been to hold a contemplative Art Oasis using seasonal themes as inspiration for creative activity. Following a bring-and-share lunch, one of our number would introduce a range of art materials and demonstrate some possible uses, before we shared in a Lectio Divina reading of a relevant Bible passage. The Lectio reading would spark ideas or images on which we would work individually, in silence, in shared space, using the materials provided. Our time would end with the showing and sharing of our work and with prayer.

Our original plans for the Lent Oasis could clearly not go ahead, so we thought initially of asking those attending to set aside, at home, the time that we would have spent together. We sent out simple instructions and timings, together with the Lectio reading, so we could all be together in time, if not in person. However, those who were more conversant with online meetings encouraged those who could to meet virtually for the demonstration of materials and shared Lectio reading. We then worked at home on the ideas sparked through the Lectio reading (some remaining online, others not) and re-gathered online for sharing, showing and prayer before ending.

Most photographed or scanned their pieces, sending these images to form a new online exhibition on the congregational Facebook page, meaning that the work from the Oasis was shared more widely than had previously been the case. The Lent Oasis was deemed so successful that an additional Oasis was organized at Pentecost, with a third virtual exhibition resulting. Our online Oasis sessions were enhanced by involvement from those in other parts of the world, including the USA and Hong Kong, as past congregation members and new friends were also able to join us.

Contemplating works of art in a group setting was also a feature of Inspired to Follow, a programme of hour-long gatherings covering the biblical story from Creation to Apocalypse. This course uses fine art paintings found in the collection of the National Gallery as a springboard for exploring ways of deepening one's Christian faith and what it means to follow Jesus today. Inspired to Follow was created at St Martin's in partnership with the National Gallery and, since the materials can be downloaded from the St Martin's website, has been used by many churches around the world.

Inspired to Follow gained a new life online during lockdown as the session format was easily deliverable in a virtual meeting space. At St Martin's we ran the whole series online, joined by people from around the globe as well as members of our congregations. Other churches also contacted us to share that they were doing the same. Sessions begin by viewing one image, which the meeting host is able to show by sharing their screen, with participants then saying what they see within the painting. This was enhanced online by the facility to zoom in to examine particular details of interest to participants. The next stages of the session, the reading of a related Bible passage and the sharing of a reflection on both painting and passage, were both easily managed in the virtual meeting using screenshare. Then came small group discussions managed virtually using the breakout room facility, with the groups brought back towards the end of the time for shared feedback and a closing prayer. Explanations of the process were also posted in the chat, as were the questions for small group discussions plus information about other future or related sessions.

Inspired to Follow was offered online as part of the Heart-Edge Living God's Future Now programme developed during lockdown. This programme of online seminars, discussions and presentations, designed to equip, encourage and energize church leaders, laypeople and enquirers, provided an opportunity to share a number of the art initiatives and approaches used at St Martin's over the years.

In Seeing Salvation – Art in Churches, we shared practical approaches to using art in church settings covering trails, contemplation, workshops, meditations, festivals, exhibitions and installations. Examples shared from St Martin's included a community art project and installation led by Anna Sikorska, an installation of 2,000 origami doves of peace, and Art Oasis workshops. Interviews with the artists Sophie Hacker and Matthew Askey explored their understandings of imaging the invisible. Sophie specializes in church art, including stained-glass windows, vestments and reordering liturgical space, while Matthew draws, paints, plays the saxophone, curates exhibitions and is also an ordained priest and chaplain.

Artists, curators and hosts from PassionArt projects shared their approaches in a workshop entitled The Art of Belonging. PassionArt aims to recover beauty at the heart of our communities through collective acts of creativity built around art and faith through exhibitions, art trails, projects, teaching, resourcing and creative gatherings. Based in Manchester, they have built links and partnerships with churches and secular cultural institutions to encourage the creative exploration of Christian festivals and to integrate faith, beauty and creative practice within the city. They aim to push creative boundaries using contemporary art and installation to visually critique our time and culture and to consider ways to increase beauty and hope in our place.

Finally, for a virtual Parish Away Day we created a wall hanging and hosted a discussion of favourite artworks. Andrew Carter oversaw the wall hanging project, creating a design based on the ceiling of the Scrovegni Chapel in Padua. This enabled everyone at the Away Day to customize a star that was later sewn onto the blue background of the hanging. Andrew recorded a video explaining the project, everyone was sent a star-shaped piece of fabric, the stars were decorated as each person wished using any appropriate materials (e.g. textiles, thread, beads, fabric paints or pens) and then returned by a designated date for sewing. The completed hanging then featured in a Sunday morning service.

In a virtual meeting we also discussed our favourite art-works, using that as an opportunity to explore

- what it is to which we are responding in works of art
- the ways artworks communicate visually
- how ideas and emotions are explored visually
- how a sense of the spiritual might have been engendered
- how the imagination of God appears in human creations.

Virtual gifts from art

While our Lent exhibition remained mothballed, our creatives remained active. Our virtual art activities enabled creative contemplation, the deepening of discipleship, and new work that was both virtual and actual. By sharing art online we discovered new ways to create as well as finding that some of our existing activities could be adapted and enhanced, especially by enabling a wider range of people to access those activities. These were our ways of finding abundance in the scarcity of a pandemic.

In an online interview during lockdown, I said:

Change begins as we think outside of the box, outside of our own perceptions. Art helps us to see differently. Artists notice things that others of us don't. That's their role; to look more attentively at life and the world than others do and to shape what they see in such a way that enables us to see what it was that the artist saw originally. As a result, artists often give us a different perspective on faith and society. By allowing us to see things differently, artists open up the possibility of change for us.

In this period the artists and craftspeople of St Martin's have been change-makers through their attentiveness to others (those already in the group and those with whom we connected online), technological opportunities (adapting and experimenting), Scripture (Inspired to Follow reflections and Oasis Lectio readings) and partnership (with individual artists around the world and with organizations such as PassionArt). Lockdown has been a time for seeing – for insight – whether creating or contemplating. From our lockdown cells we have learnt again that the kind of close contemplative looking that is fundamental to art when 'taken to its highest degree' is, as the philosopher Simone Weil said, 'the same thing as prayer'.[1] We responded to lockdown by creating contemplative moments online, enabling those who wished to pay prayerful attention to the present moment.

Through lockdown I realized, first, as we already knew from the growth of digital art, that when creatives use new technology, unexpected outcomes emerge. The many online exhibitions that artists, galleries, museums, journals, churches, chaplains and cathedrals have created have often been fascinating in content, directly inspired by pandemic experiences and innovative in their presentation of the art itself. Second, creativity itself has been revealed, once again, as one of the best coping mechanisms available to us as human beings because it is an outlet for expression of what is within. We all know that bottling up emotions, because they fester within, is as counter-productive as simply expressing all we feel in one big splurge. The arts help us to express emotions in ways that are channelled as we shape them to be shared with others. That process is one that enables us to reflect on our experiences, not simply to express them. The more we all learn to tap our inherent God-given creativity, whatever our gifts may be, the more they can become a means to help us cope with the challenging experiences that life throws in our path.

Finally, I also realized that artists are one of the groups in society whose regular practice involves elements of withdrawal and isolation. In relation to inspiration and creativity that is their choice – their experience is different from the enforced restrictions of lockdown. Yet their experience of how to use

---

1 Simone Weil, *Gravity and Grace* (London: Routledge, 2004), p. 117.

isolation and withdrawal for creative ends holds out significant opportunities for society to learn ways to cope and make productive use of the lockdown experience, which seems as though it is likely to be a feature of life for some time to come. We are not good, either as church or as society, at identifying those within our midst who already having the experience and knowledge needed for the situation we are facing; but that is what God in his abundance always provides. We need to be more attuned to recognize the gifts God has sent, which we have overlooked. Artists are among those gifts.

Art Oasis format

Sarah Sikorska, our Art Oasis organizer, prepared the following instructions for the Pentecost Art Oasis.

PENTECOST SUNDAY OASIS 2020
Dear Friends at St Martin's and others,

As we are no longer able to meet together for times of Art Oasis, this is an invitation to do something in our own homes at the same time on Pentecost Sunday so that we can reflect and create together as a wider Oasis community; by doing so we can support and encourage each other in prayer.

For those who have not attended an Art Oasis before, I will just say a few words about the process that we follow. We normally gather together for a shared lunch and then listen to the scripture passage for that day. We hear it three times, with a time of silence in between each reading. The listening and the silence help us to engage and respond.

During the second time of listening, we might find a word or image that comes to our attention that is helpful to stay with. During the third time of listening (or reading in this case) we are able to rest with, ponder upon and deepen whatever draws our attention.

In the shared silence we then move to the art materials. We can spend a period of time (however long we want) using whatever materials are at hand, to express, play with, illustrate, explore and discover that which holds us from the passage.

The important thing is to suspend judgement – either self-criticism or memories of a discouraging art teacher. By being alone we can feel free to do what we want. We can be led by God's creativity.

Art materials

What have we got at home? If we just have a pencil or biro, so be it. Maybe we can find some crayons, pastels or a paint box or some glue and coloured paper or tissue paper and scissors. Magazines and newspapers throw up a multitude of printed words and images and even colours, textures and patterns we may wish to use. Use them, cut them out, tear them, paint over them, stick them down, scrunch them up – have fun!

I always find that *starting* any art process is the hardest part. So, if we know that we are starting together at 2pm this Sunday 31 May, we may find it easier. If we are late, no worries, we can do it anytime. Maybe, before you begin, put any materials you have on a table.

So, let's begin. Here is the reading for Pentecost Sunday – Acts 2.1–21.

Finishing

When we have finished our pieces we can take time to reflect on the experience.

We offer thanks for all that we have been given,
for our shared endeavour
and for grace bestowed.
We pray for each other, both near and far,
remembering that we are always held
in God's loving hands. Amen.

Resources

'Inspired to Follow: Art and the Bible Story', www.stmartin-in-the-fields.org/life-st-martins/discipleship/inspired-to-follow/, accessed 30.11.2020.

'Seeing Salvation – Art in churches' and 'Imaging the Invisible', www.facebook.com/theHeartEdge/videos/?ref=page_internal, accessed 30.11.2020.

PassionArt resource pack, www.passionart.guide/keep-in-touch/, accessed 30.11.2020.

'Change begins with art' interview, www.facebook.com/allwecanuk/videos/356579665312352, accessed 30.11.2020.

8

Hearing Scripture Together in Difficult Times

RICHARD CARTER AND
CATHERINE DUCE

Many years ago I remember being inspired by *The Gospel in Solentiname*. Solentiname is an archipelago on Lake Nicaragua where Ernesto Cardenal – poet, priest, radical activist and later politician – recorded the conversations of his community each Sunday. Instead of having a sermon, they would enter into dialogue and commentary on the Gospel for the day. These commentaries were carried out by *campesinos* – farmers, labourers and fishermen. Cardenal writes that these commentaries 'are usually of greater profundity than that of many theologians, but have a simplicity like that of the Gospel itself. This is not surprising,' he says, 'for the *Gospel* or "Good News" to the poor was written for them.'[1] Cardenal notes the different people who took part in these commentaries and the themes or insights that were closest to each of their hearts: there was Marcello the mystic; Rebeca, who always stresses love; Elvis, longing for a more just society; Felipe, conscious of the struggle of the poorest; Old Tomas, who can't read but speaks with great wisdom; Alejandro, who delivers speeches for others' benefit; Panco, who is conservative; Julio, a greater defender of equality; and Oscar, who longs for a greater unity. Each of these voices is distinct and has something to share, and yet it is the coming together of these lived perspectives

---

1 Ernesto Cardenal, *The Gospel in Solentiname, Volume 4* (New York: Orbis, 1982), p. vii.

that creates the *Gospel of Solentiname*: Christ's gospel, but earthed in their time and place, and responding to each of their needs. Let me give you a brief example. Here they comment on Mary's Magnificat:

'My soul praises the Lord, my heart rejoices in God my Saviour, because he has noticed his slave.'

'She praises God because the Messiah is going to be born, and that's a great event for the people.'

'She calls God "Saviour" because she knows that the Son that he has given her is going to bring liberation.'

'She's full of joy. Us women must also be that way, because in our community the Messiah is born too, the liberator.'

'She recognizes liberation ... We have to do the same thing. Liberation is from sin, that is, from selfishness, from injustice, from misery, from ignorance – from everything that's oppressive. That liberation is in our wombs too, it seems to me ...'

The last speaker was Andrea, a young married woman, and now Oscar, her young husband, breaks in: 'God is selfish because he wants us to be his slaves. He wants our submission. Just him. I don't see why Mary has to call herself a slave. We should be free! Why just him? That's selfishness.'

Alejandro: 'We have to be slaves of God, not of men.'

Another young man: 'God is love. To be a slave of love is to be free because God doesn't make slaves. He's the only thing we should be slaves of, love. And then we don't make slaves of others.'

Alejandro's mother says: 'To be a slave of God is to serve others. That slavery is liberation.'

I said that it's true that this selfish God Oscar spoke about does exist. And it's a God invented by people. People have often invented a god in their own image and likeness – not the true God, but idols, and those religions are alienating. But the God of the Bible does not teach religion, but rather he urges Moses to take Israel out of Egypt, where the Jews were working as slaves: 'To set my people free.'[2]

---

2 Ernesto Cardenal, *The Gospel in Solentiname*, *Volume 1* (New York: Orbis, 1976), pp. 34–5.

In these commentaries the gospel comes alive. Notice how each of their comments has an individual language, but also a shared language of their group, and a language of their context and time. The common theme is liberation, but each person is making that liberation their own. Sam Wells writes,

> Before the Bible became a vehicle for private devotion, encased in leather and cocooned by a zip, it was a script for perform- ance, a rallying cry for mission, a tirade seeking repentance and a chorus of comfort. It was a community-forming sacra- ment, and reading it aloud was a church-creating event. It did not have a static meaning; it was not reduced to easily memorized fundamentals. Every time it was read aloud in a congregation its truth became new in the context of its hearers, and every time the hearers returned to listen again they were a new and different community to the one that had heard it before.[3]

In this way not only does Scripture transform us, but we trans- form Scripture.

When Jesus stands up in the synagogue and says, 'Today this Scripture has been fulfilled in your hearing' (Luke 4.21), he is giving one of not only the shortest sermons ever preached but also the most effective. This is the model of how Scripture should be read. We are being called to enter into it. How is the Scripture being fulfilled here and now, in me and my life, in this church, in my community or nation or world? The Scripture is only complete when word becomes flesh. We are not dispensing 'oven-ready' solutions or methods of control. We are entering into a text like a swimmer entering into the water and into depths that will always be greater than us. This is the spirit of Hans Urs von Balthasar, who calls for us not to regard Scripture as a fact or object. Rather:

---

3 Richard Carter and Samuel Wells, 'Holy Theatre: Enfleshing the Word' in *Theatrical Theology: Explorations in Performing the Faith*, edited by Wesley Vander Lugt and Trevor Hart (Eugene, OR: Cascade, 2014), p. 224.

We must allow the encountering reality to speak its own tongue, let ourselves be drawn into the dramatic arena. For God's revelation is not an object to be looked at: it is an action in and upon the world, and the world can only respond, and hence understand through action on its part.[4]

In this time of pandemic and uncertainty we too have found the gospel coming alive, in the life of our community and beyond, in new and unexpected ways. When something in our lives is at stake, the reading of Scripture is no longer an intellectual or detached exercise – it involves what's happening now and how we make sense of the greatest issues of our lives. What do we believe in? What will hold us together through a time of trial? How do we love? How do we share? How do we forgive, how do we live together? Ultimately, how do we face our mortality and approach our death? This suddenly makes much more sense because we too have entered into Christ's story, and like *The Gospel of Solentiname* we are hearing the gospel together and seeking to become gospel for our times.

Lectio Divina

We need to discover a pattern and a way of entering into Scripture so that it ceases to be an exercise in who knows the most about the text, and becomes a way of inhabiting the text – or to use Christ's image, the text becoming for us the 'bread of life'. In order to do this, the traditional practice of divine reading or Lectio Divina is helpful. I have described this process in *The City is My Monastery: A Contemporary Rule of Life*:

The method
The text is seen as a gift to be received
The passage of Scripture is read slowly
It is given time and space

---

4 Hans Urs von Balthasar, *Theo-Drama: Theological Dramatic Theory, Volume 1* (Ignatius Press 1983), p. 15.

It is allowed to filter into our own life and context
It is repeated, each reading taking us deeper
The text questions us and opens possibility
It is a means of discovering God
It is a means of discovering our hidden selves
The movement

In the twelfth century, the Carthusian monk, Guigo, described the four movements of Lectio Divina as:

1 Reading: selecting the sacred text and listening to it speak to you.
2 Meditating: a deep entry into the meaning of the text.
3 Praying: the reader's response to God in the light of this reading.
4 Contemplating: resting or living in the presence of God.

Guigo uses the image of eating to illustrate these different stages of digesting a text:

1 Reading selects the food and puts it into the mouth.
2 Meditation chews it and breaks it open.
3 Prayer extracts its flavour.
4 Contemplation is the sweetness itself which gladdens and refreshes.[5]

In our own practice of Lectio during the pandemic our means of meeting has needed to accommodate fast-changing government guidelines: the Lectio has been conducted via Zoom and the internet or, when allowed, in small groups of six people meeting together. We read the passage three times. After the second reading each person in the group is invited to identify a word, sentence or idea that seems to be speaking to them or challenging them. After the third reading, each person has the chance to reflect or comment upon the word they have chosen. As described in *The Gospel of Solentiname*, each person who

---

5 Richard Carter, *The City is My Monastery: A Contemporary Rule of Life* (Norwich: Canterbury Press, 2019), pp. 99–103.

contributes brings their own story, context and themes to bear. A composite larger narrative can often emerge that includes all our stories. S, for example, brings a story of childhood exclusion that still haunts her in this pandemic; P brings his experience of homelessness, where there is no place to self-isolate; D brings her anxiety about her husband's illness, made more intense by the crisis; and G relates the story of how so many have been socially isolated because of disability that she herself experiences; long before Covid-19, D brings a haunting memory of the past and the realization that it is only this shared gospel that is holding his head above water.

After everyone has had the opportunity to speak, we move to a time of wondering. Three wonderings are chosen, grounded in the scriptural passage for the day. These wonderings create space for the Spirit to speak into our situations. A wondering is not a question; it is an opening-into – a door through which we can enter a deeper landscape of our lives and our times. (A list of all the Scripture passages and wonderings used in lockdown is at the end of this chapter.) We read the text and the text reads us. Not only is the text revealed but we are revealed in the text – and, what is more, Christ is revealed in us. There is a healing power in this that is difficult to describe. As George Herbert writes, Scripture 'is the well that washes what it shows':

O Book! infinite sweetness! let my heart
Suck ev'ry letter, and a honey gain,
Precious for any grief in any part;
To clear the breast, to mollify all pain.
Thou art all health, health thriving till it make
A full eternity: thou art a mass
Of strange delights, where we may wish and take.[6]

We end our time together in prayer, gathering all these experiences before God, in which we recognize the sacredness of all that has been shared. What we are perceiving is that each of us,

---

6 George Herbert, *The Complete Poetry*, edited by John Drury and Victoria Moul (London: Penguin 2015), pp. 56–7.

in responding to the gospel in our hearts, can speak gospel ourselves. There is a power in naming and recognizing in prayer what has taken place. Through prayer we uphold with open hands all we have shared – like the boy who brings his fish and barley loaves to Christ. In prayer our offering is blessed and shared, and we recognize that we have all been fed. Our offerings and sharings become our prayer. We have dared to reveal both our hunger and our offering. Many people acknowledge that this is the moment in their week where they feel most open and most listened to and where they feel able to voice their deepest self. This spirit of non-judgemental listening is so valued in our city today and our trust deepens week by week.

Here is a short example of our Gospel for Trafalgar Square in the time of pandemic. We ask a frontline nurse who works in a coronavirus ward to choose a passage of Scripture that has spoken to her during the crisis. She chooses Isaiah 43.1–10:

> Do not fear, for I have redeemed you;
> I have called you by name, you are mine.
> When you pass through the waters, I will be with you;
> and through the rivers, they shall not overwhelm you;
> when you walk through fire you shall not be burned,
> and the flame shall not consume you.

In church this nurse reflects, and afterwards this honest testimony of someone living through an acutely real situation opens the hearts of those carrying their own unresolved stories and experiences. No longer are we looking at clever ways to interpret Isaiah's words: we are struggling to understand or accept the truths they are disclosing to us now. It is shared as a second wave of the virus in the UK gathers pace and anxieties are high.

The full passage is read three times.

> But now thus says the Lord,
> he who created you, O Jacob,
> he who formed you, O Israel:
> Do not fear, for I have redeemed you;
> I have called you by name, you are mine.

When you pass through the waters, I will be with you;
and through the rivers, they shall not overwhelm you;
when you walk through fire you shall not be burned,
and the flame shall not consume you.
For I am the Lord your God,
the Holy One of Israel, your Saviour.
I give Egypt as your ransom,
Ethiopia and Seba in exchange for you.
Because you are precious in my sight,
and honoured, and I love you,
I give people in return for you,
nations in exchange for your life.
Do not fear, for I am with you;
I will bring your offspring from the east,
and from the west I will gather you;
I will say to the north, 'Give them up',
and to the south, 'Do not withhold;
bring my sons from far away
and my daughters from the end of the earth –
everyone who is called by my name,
whom I created for my glory,
whom I formed and made.'
Bring forth the people who are blind, yet have eyes,
who are deaf, yet have ears!
Let all the nations gather together,
and let the peoples assemble.
Who among them declared this,
and foretold to us the former things?
Let them bring their witnesses to justify them,
and let them hear and say, 'It is true.'
You are my witnesses, says the Lord,
and my servant whom I have chosen,
so that you may know and believe me
and understand that I am he.
Before me no god was formed,
nor shall there be any after me.

Chosen words and responses

A participant from the disability conference: Does it just have to be positive things I mention? I really don't like the idea of God sacrificing all these people. If Egypt is your ransom and Ethiopia and Seba in exchange for you. All these other humans are just lost and gone. I can't say I'm comfortable with that, how could anyone be? But I like the idea of people who the world thinks of as 'unvisioned' actually being some of the best visionaries and people who the world thinks of as deaf actually being some of the best listeners.

A parishioner: 'I will gather you.' I am feeling no small measure of frustration and sadness at not being able to travel and be at St Martin's to be able to be with my friends and to be of service to other people in a very practical way and yet there is something so extraordinary about the way that God gathers us together and through prayer and through holding other people in our hearts there is an amazing sense of connection. I am so relishing this time of opportunity to be with you all this evening. In prayer and worship earlier on it was so powerful. I love the 'peace be with you'. That's my favourite moment when we are connecting online. I feel as if everyone is sharing the peace with everyone else, which has an even wider dimension online with people gathering from across the nation and world than in a service in person where you only share peace with one or two people around you. So I just feeling blessed by this extraordinary sense of gathering as Christians gather from all around the world in all their diversity.

An ordinand: 'Do not withhold.' The passage talked about gathering. Bring my sons from far away and my daughters from the end of the earth, everyone who is called by my name. God says, Do not withhold. I suppose it made me think about withholding. How much we withhold and how much I withhold in our own life and in the life of the church. What causes us to withhold? What makes us hold back? What stops us from giving everything that we have got? What stops us from widening the scope of our vision as far as we can widen it? I guess it strikes me it requires quite a lot of courage not to hold anything back. To truly recognize the sons and daughters that are far away and at the end of the earth and called by the name of God. Sometimes there is a social pressure to withhold and people who let everything out and are really free-flowing are called enthusiastic. So an interesting idea that God tells us not to hold anything back, and what does that look like.

A Companion of Nazareth: 'I have called you by name, you are mine.' I find this line wonderfully reassuring in my loneliness and solitude.

Someone who works for the church: 'You are my witnesses, says the Lord, and my servant whom I have chosen.' Essentially this whole passage is so soaked in goodness. Almost like a blanket you want to wrap around you, that you want to hide under and feel safe and feel the protection of these words. But actually 'You are my witnesses' stuck out to me because we can't just hide under the blanket and think we are safe. We are called to go out as a chosen people, to go out and tell people that we are precious, honoured and loved. The message is quite simple. Yet the church gets caught up in management-speak and mission initiatives, when, in fact, ministry is simply about drawing alongside people and communicating to them that they are special in the eyes of God. I needed that reminder tonight. It's so simple it's complicated to do, if you know what I mean!

Wonderings

- I wonder how God is calling you.
- I wonder where you find God's healing in your life.
- I wonder where you see healing in the world around you, particularly since the arrival of Covid-19.

I think the bit that is sticking out to me is I wonder how God is calling you. Well, I wonder how God is calling me! I've so many excuses. I perhaps haven't given God much time to listen. I think something is going to change but what? I can't figure that one out yet. It would be quite nice if God wrote me a letter or wrote a big letter in the sky saying, 'X, you know you are going this way, don't you.' But no!

I am being called into some sort of solitary life. Part of that is settling into a particular place in these times of Covid, rather than a nomadic lifestyle where I'm free to go wherever God is sending me. This is an entry into place, and staying with place, that I have never known before.

I find healing in God's forgiveness and in forgiving myself. An absolution I love from my previous church are these words: 'God forgives you, forgive others, forgive yourself.' I find God's healing at the moment flourishing most in the sense that forgiving myself is as important as any other forgiveness that I might give or receive.

I'm finding wonderful nourishment and healing in the Nazareth Rule of Life. It is really helping me. I am trying to spend time in the silence. I feel it is a new and living way. It is helping me hugely. My husband died and I felt very jagged and adrift but somehow this is helping me hugely.

I find healing in one another in these groups and in the fellowship of these groups. I really do. Who would think but after a group like this I feel I have heard and been heard.

Healing is found in unexpected places and when we are least expecting it. On a hospital chaplaincy placement I remember we took communion to a girl in her twenties on a ward and she was about to have a really big operation – she was about to undergo irreversible surgery – there was a real sense of brokenness and fear about her but we shared a brief service together and gave her communion. I just remember *seeing* a real sense of healing in her. It was a really powerful experience. I could see healing happening.

It's strange, isn't it, how deeply those who work for the NHS have moved this nation and become part of our shared narrative. What is it about them – their compassion? Their healing? Their putting their own life at risk? The fact that they are on the frontline and have faced pain and death? Their sacrifice to save other people's lives? These values are familiar to us. They are all Christlike qualities at the very heart of the gospel. It has taken the NHS to make the Word flesh for us.

I believe it is not too extreme to say that our Lectio groups in lockdown have anchored people in a storm. They have held people in their distress. They have walked with people in their anxieties and darkness. And through listening to one another light has shone through the cracks. The Lectio groups have been a path of transformation. As we listen to one another, a deeper truth emerges that is more than the sum of all of us. Through listening to the gospel together, a community has been born, which enriches us well beyond the group itself.

Bread for the World in lockdown: Scriptures and wonderings

Living resurrection now – Luke 24.35–48

- I wonder how these days of lockdown are changing you.
- I wonder how your body experiences resurrection now (eyes, heart, hands, feet, wounds).
- I wonder where in your life you most need to hear the words 'Peace be with you.'

Fleeing, fighting, staying, loving – John 21.15–19

- I wonder what we want to flee from.
- I wonder what we want to fight for.
- I wonder what we want to stay with.
- I wonder what we love.

Waiting, trusting, surrendering – John 12.24–27

- I wonder what God might be inviting you to surrender.
- I wonder what fears are arising in you at this time of waiting and not knowing.
- I wonder what your transformed life might look like.

Interrupting silence – Mark 7.24–30

- I wonder when your assumptions have been called into question by an outsider.
- I wonder what the difference is between a listening silence and an oppressive silence.
- I wonder which silences need to be broken today to share the Good News.

Christian Aid Week – Luke 10.25–37

- I wonder what social distancing means to you.
- I wonder where you are in the story of the Good Samaritan.
- I wonder where you see signs of the kingdom of God in our world.

If they keep quiet the stones will cry out – Luke 19.37–46

- I wonder when you have been inspired by love and anger.
- I wonder how we should respond to the injustices and prejudice of continuing racial discrimination.
- I wonder what in our world makes you weep and I wonder what makes you shout with joy.

Pilgrimage – John 3.1–16

- I wonder what pilgrimage means to you.
- I wonder whether you have experienced any 'pilgrimage' moments in the current lockdown.
- I wonder where and in what circumstances you have had personal encounters with the free 'wind' of the Spirit.

Finding God in lockdown – Matthew 6.25–34

- I wonder what has been the struggle of lockdown.
- I wonder what for you has been the blessing of lockdown.
- I wonder if you have known what it feels like to be set free.

Listening to build community – Romans 12.1–8

- I wonder who are the unheard and unseen in your community.
- I wonder if there was a time when listening changed you.
- I wonder what it feels like to be heard.

Freedom in South Africa; young people of St Mary's Cathedral, Johannesburg – Luke 4.16–21

- I wonder what struck you about the voices of young people from South Africa tonight.
- I wonder what we are doing as a church to promote UBUNTU.
- I wonder in your own life where you long for freedom.

Welcoming new members of the Nazareth Community – Matthew 26.36–45

- Tell about a time when you stopped and others went on.
- Tell about a time when others stopped and you carried on.
- I wonder whether right now you are at the edge of the garden or in the middle.

The spirituality of the sea – Mark 4.35–41

- I wonder how the sea speaks to you spiritually.
- I wonder how God has been present to you in a storm.
- I wonder with whom you could share the words 'Peace! Be still!' over the coming week.

The power of story – Psalm 78.1–8

- I wonder what your favourite story is and what it has taught you about yourself.
- I wonder whether you have a favourite Bible story. I wonder what you learn about yourself from it.
- I wonder whether you have ever felt like a bystander in your own story.
- I wonder whether you prefer to look back to your old stories or to create new ones.

Noticing and naming the creativity of God – Genesis 1.1–3, 27–28, 31a; 2.1–2, 19–20

- I wonder what you have noticed in the course of today.
- I wonder what you named for yourself or others in the course of today.
- I wonder how you express your creativity.

9

Discerning the Wisdom
of Prophetic Lives

CATHERINE DUCE AND
RICHARD CARTER

Thomas Merton once said that all of us should aspire to become saints. Before we quickly count ourselves out, perhaps it's worth realizing that saints are not saints because of what they do, but because of what God does through them. In his 2020 autumn lecture at St Martin-in-the-Fields, 'Trusting in God', Rowan Williams spoke of the importance of trusting in the shared narratives of our faith that can bring hope in a time of struggle and despair. What are those narratives for today? Rowan Williams cited our raising up of the NHS. No one is saying that all NHS staff are saints, but through their lives they inspire us with a vision of a greater humanity: compassion, sacrificial service, the healing of the sick and a willingness to put their own lives on the line for the good of others. Each one of those characteristics is a gospel value. We all need narratives of hope, and during this time we have also rediscovered some of the shared stories of our Christian faith. The insights from the spiritual wisdom of mystics, martyrs and saints, who themselves have lived through times of trial, danger and adversity, have enhanced our understanding of our own faith. As we have reflected on their lives and writing, we have seen how our Christian tradition is a not a linear progression but a constant spiral in which we seek and are sought by God. 'If I am lost tell them I will be found by love' (St John of the Cross). Here are just a few examples of the cloud of witnesses who have been helping us through the pandemic.

St Benedict

For 1,500 years the Rule of St Benedict[1] has been one of the most influential texts in living the Christian life. It's not just for monks, but for us here and now. The Rule of St Benedict is a call to action. We often think of the monastic life as a retreat and an escape into silence and solitude or even passivity. But it's not at all, and it takes on a new relevance when we too are forced to restructure our lives and values. Look at the words of the prologue with which we are addressed. Benedict tells us to listen, labour, do battle, run, seek, respond, get up, and arise from sleep. Those who come to the monastery are not seeking escape or turning their back on the rigours of the world. This is an active school, in which the monk is called to turn to God with a strong sense of urgency, recognizing that on our own we are in serious trouble. This is a call to realign our lives and depend upon God's grace.

The rule provides the framework through which we turn to Christ in all things and through which God's grace can flow. These structures are the banks through which to channel the water. If there is no water, of course, those banks are useless: but if there are no banks, the water does not reach us. Just as we have discussed in our reading of Scripture, in a time of uncertainty this text comes alive. What strikes you when you read the Prologue is that Benedict believes our very life, our salvation, is at stake. Benedict wants to establish the habits, disciplines and service of a way of life that is going to lead to true conversion. He prepares us for a long journey. He wants to set out good sustainable practice: a practice that will allow God to do what needs to be done in our lives, for all of our lives. This is not a flash-in-the-pan burst of inspiration. Benedict is in it for the long haul. He is taking the gospel as his guide; and that call to conversion is rigorous. But there is also compassion and gentleness. This is not an intransigent rule. This is the rule of 'a father who loves you'. Obedience is not a form of oppression, but a deeper way of listening.

---

1 See www.solesmes.com/sites/default/files/upload/pdf/rule_of_st_benedict.pdf, accessed 14.2.2021.

For example, the abbot is called upon to lead and to point out what is good and holy more by action than by words. Benedict calls upon the abbot to show equal love for everyone and judge not by the ranks of society. And while the monks are called upon to be obedient to the abbot in all things, it is in the knowledge that the abbot will be held to account for the souls given into his care. He calls for a compassion and care for the poor: 'you must relieve the lot of the poor, clothe the naked, visit the sick and bury the dead. Go to help the troubled and console the sorrowful.' He calls for honesty and integrity: 'the love of Christ must come before all else. You are not to act in anger or nurse a grudge. Rid your heart of all deceit. Never give a hollow greeting of peace or turn away when someone needs your love. Speak the truth with heart and tongue.' He has special concern for the elderly, the young, the infirm, the guest at the door, in the receiving of the poor and pilgrims in whom we see Christ. 'In drawing up its regulations we hope to set down nothing harsh, nothing burdensome. The good of all concerned however may prompt us to a little strictness in order to amend faults and to safeguard love.'

How important each of the above is in the leadership and disciplines that we need to get us through this period of our history. What can we learn from this Rule? Perhaps there is in all of us this longing for God, this thirst that we have experienced but never quenched. I have seen this in so many people: someone who has tasted or experienced the love of God, and longs to follow that path. In this last year have we not tasted again this same longing? Those moments when we realize that there is something more important than the place our frantic search to keep up, compete and succeed has led us to?

Fleeing

There is in many of us a longing to find sanctuary and rest, and to find a secure place of belonging. Perhaps in our own armoury we have stored away an escape route, a plan, a sacred place, a retreat that can help us as we imagine a way out of our own overwhelming circumstances. Yet perhaps this longing is not so much an escape but a calling to re-establish God's time. Walter Brueggemann talks about 'Sabbath as Resistance'. Finding a way of rediscovering God's reality – attentiveness in the midst of a culture that feels inhospitable to our faith; finding our identity. How can I overcome my anxieties, overcome my fears and become more God-centred? How can I rediscover the priorities of my life by which to live? How can I discover meaning that makes sense of my own narrative? How can I live more authentically? How can I, facing the knowledge of my mortality, make eternal choices?

Fighting

Not long after the fleeing comes the realization that our demons have not been left behind but have followed us. We notice the same movement in the Desert Fathers. The desert, far from being the place of escape, becomes the place of confrontation where we come face to face with our own humanity, and are forced to renounce diversion – and, in the words of Thomas Merton, 'heal in ourselves the sins of the world'. How many of us, for all our good intentions and resolutions, found the place of solitude not the peaceful place we thought it would be? Fleeing the ways of the world involves in the prodigal a painful coming to one's senses. The escape is not an escape at all, but a painful awakening. For many of us this has been the experience of the pandemic. The encounter with God frees us from the masks that we wear – the conformity and the prejudices – and forces us to question the values by which we live.

It is perhaps only later that we begin to experience this sense of overwhelming not as loss but as transformation – indeed as our own Pentecost. Perhaps our awakening to the call of God is not a monastery at all, but a doctor's waiting room, or a hospital bedside, or a relationship of deep unfathomable love and pain, or a realization of sin and failure, or an encounter with goodness or beauty through a journey when we learnt to trust.

I wonder where the place is in your life when you have been surprised by God or overwhelmed by your need of God. I wonder when you realized more than ever before that you wanted to listen carefully to the master's instructions and attend to them with the ear of your heart – to learn in the school of the Lord's service.

Finding

This is not a fleeing from the world, but a dwelling in the world. Benedict believed in stability, which is still one of the Benedictine vows. This perseverance, this steadfastness, is as important to faith as perseverance is to a mountain climber. It is at the very point that we come up against aridity, temptation and conflict that we should hold fast to our discipline and not abandon it in fear. It is by suffering the indignity of our present imperfection that we allow grace to work its wonders in its own good time. It is in perseverance in the Lord's service into the unknown and our regular patient commitment to God that we begin to discover a greater freedom than we have hitherto known. Benedict writes, 'As we progress in the way of life and in faith, we shall run on the path of the Lord's Commandments, our hearts overflowing with inexpressible delights of love.'

Julian of Norwich

In her *Revelations of Divine Love*, written during the terrifying time of the Black Death and Hundred Years War, Julian of Norwich, the fourteenth-century anchoress who lived a life of seclusion and prayer, wrote this revelation of trust:

And the Lord showed me a little thing, the size of a hazelnut, on the palm of my hand, round like a ball. I looked at it thoughtfully and wondered 'What is this?' And the answer came. 'It is all that is made.' I marvelled that it continued to exist and did not suddenly disintegrate; it was so small. And again my mind supplied the answer. 'It exists both now and forever, because God loves it.' In short everything owes its existence to the love of God. In this little thing I saw three truths. The first is that God made it, the second is that God loves it and the third is that God sustains it.[2]

This may sound a very simple insight. But for our community at this time it has proved a profound one. One of the most important things about being a church on the edge of Trafalgar Square in the middle of London in these times of uncertainty is to hold fast to these truths.

First, God made us. How often it seems that we are of our own making our own becoming. We can control our lives and they are our inventions, as it were. One of the greatest and most painful lessons of this time is to learn that we are mortal. During this time we have had to place our lives in the hands of our creator: offering ourselves like a seed in the dark soil of unknowing yet knowing that God is the one who gives life.

Second, God loves us. The love of God is the source of all our flourishing, our growing, our meaning. The temptation that will constantly be at work in our lives is the temptation that casts doubt on that love. This doubt will whisper that you are unworthy, that you are the reject, that you do not belong or that you are the outcast. But God is love. All the Scriptures are read to hear that love between the lines and any interpretation of the Bible where you cannot hear that voice of love is not to be trusted. Our Christian faith means nothing if we do not live out of that love. We do not make God known by fear or by argument but only ultimately by love.

Third, God sustains us. We cannot control or fully predict what someone we care about will become. We cannot force someone to love. From Jesus Christ we learn the meaning of that sustaining love. It is not something that is grabbed or taken, but a love that is offered, it does not condemn or dictate, but longs for fullness of life. The life that seems small, precarious, seemingly hopeless – the voice of wisdom and love speaking to

2 Julian of Norwich, *Revelations of Divine Love* (Penguin Classics, 1966), chapters 5–6.

the Church the message of the gospel. And when the Church listens to that voice of God's love then it awakens, it casts off the grave cloths that bind it, and becomes the Church of God's love. Made by God, loved by God, sustained by God. Perhaps it is now, in this time of uncertainty and so much fear, that the Church can find its true being – the pearl of great price that it has both to receive and to share. The mustard seed can become the tree in which all can find a place to dwell.

St John of the Cross

On 14 December 1591, just before midnight, St John of the Cross lay dying. His final request to the friars at his bedside was for them to read him a passage from the Song of Songs – a text that speaks of a deep mystical union of love, echoing the divine love story of Yahweh for Israel, a love story of Christ for his Church, and love story of Christ for each and every soul. While listening, St John of the Cross was heard to say, 'So beautiful are the flowers!'[3] And then he died.

In his life and poetry St John of the Cross testifies to a God who is a lover, longing for relationship with us, longing to meet us and to love us in our deepest hour of need. 'If a person is seeking God,' writes John, 'his beloved is seeking him much more.'[4]

Many of us carry confused and unhelpful images of God within us: images from childhood perhaps, of a God who punishes and judges, of a God as a lawgiver, whom we seek to please for our own salvation. There is little intimacy in such images; no movement or delight. St John of the Cross can help us recover an understanding of God 'as the flame of love that purifies, wounds and burns in order to lead us into something totally new: the ecstasy of love and a peace that surpasses

---

3 See www.spiritualityandpractice.com/practices/naming-the-days/view/24514/feast-day-of-st-john-of-the-cross, accessed 14.2.2021.

4 *Living Flame* (second redaction) 3.28, quoted in Iain Matthew, *The Impact of God: Soundings from St John of the Cross* (London: Hodder, 1995), p. 35. By kind permission of the Sisters of Mercy of Australia and Papua New Guinea.

human understanding'.[5] 'Open the door of your hearts,' writes John. 'Let this Lover into your being.'[6]

'The Living Flame of Love' is considered John's most personal of poems – his own 'Magnificat'[7] – in which he writes of being transformed in love's fire. Here we meet a profoundly active God: a God who anticipates, initiates, gives and transforms like a flame entering and magnifying John's heart until God engages the 'deepest centre' of his soul.[8] This is not a passive God. 'Love is never idle,' writes John. 'It is in continual movement',[9] ever new and daring, ever seeking an opening and a fresh beginning. This poem captures God's eagerness to belong to each one of us; a God whose self-giving and self-outpouring is passionate.

> Flame, alive, compelling,
> yet tender past all telling,
> reaching the secret centre of my soul!
> Since now evasion's over,
> finish your work, my Lover,
> break the last thread, wound me and make me whole!
>
> Burn that is for my healing!
> Wound of delight past feeling!
> Ah, gentle hand whose touch is a caress,
> foretaste of heaven conveying
> and every debt repaying:
> slaying, you give me life for death's distress.
>
> O lamps of fire bright-burning
> with splendid brilliance, turning
> deep caverns of my soul to pools of light!

---

5 Matthew, *The Impact of God*, p. xi.

6 Matthew, *The Impact of God*, p. xi.

7 Federico Ruiz, 'Cimas de contemplación', *Ephemerides Carmeliticae* 13 (1962), p. 268, quoted in Matthew, *The Impact of God*, p. 25.

8 Matthew, *The Impact of God*, p. 24.

9 *Living Flame* (second redaction) 1.8, quoted in Matthew, *The Impact of God*, p. 25.

Once shadowed, dim, unknowing,
now their strange new-found glowing
gives warmth and radiance for my Love's delight.

Ah! Gentle and so loving
you wake within me, proving
that you are there in secret and alone;
your fragrant breathing stills me
your grace, your glory fills me
so tenderly your love becomes my own.[10]

The imagery here is physical, sensual and passionate. This is the language of sexual intimacy and consummation. God presses in, God hovers until finding an entrance, and then burns with healing, finds the deepest core of the human person – 'turning deep caverns of the soul to pools of light'. John's understanding of God is never domesticated. God is not some object out there to be objectified and defined by doctrine. Rather, God is a living relationship with an inexpressible mystery that is both near to us and beyond all our imaginings. The dark night becomes the place of love's intimate disclosure. 'Fasten your eyes on Christ alone, and you will discover even more than you ask for and desire ...'[11]

On his deathbed St John of the Cross knew just such a self-outpouring God. Eternity meant to him love set free. That was where the night was leading.

Set me as a seal upon your heart,
as a seal upon your arm;
for love is strong as death,
passion fierce as the grave.
Its flashes are flashes of fire,
a raging flame.[12]

---

10 Matthew, *The Impact of God*, p. 23.With kind permission of Marjorie Flower OCD of the Carmelite nuns of Varroville, Australia.

11 St John of the Cross, *The Ascent of Mount Carmel*, chapter 22, 5–6. See https://aleteia.org/2017/09/22/discover-the-crucifix-drawn-by-saint-john-of-the-cross-after-a-mystical-vision/, accessed 14.2.2021.

12 Revelation 8.6.

Charles de Foucauld

On the surface, the life of priest and hermit Charles de Foucauld in the early twentieth century seems very remote from ours. Here is a man with a fierce monastic austerity, whose life culminated in a ministry among the Muslim Tuareg people in the harsh Saharan desert. In fact, by most people's standards today Charles' life was a failure. He had a difficult childhood. He was a diffident military officer who became a Trappist monk only to leave the order after seven years because it wasn't austere enough for him. He then became a solitary missionary in Algeria where he baptized only a few people in a dozen years. Some people even think his martyrdom in 1916 was a mistake.

And yet, Charles de Foucauld's understanding of the essence of the life of Jesus, which he quietly lived out and to which he witnessed, is profound and transformative. 'I think it's my vocation,' Charles writes, 'to go downward.'[13] 'For me, I always seek the lowest of the low places, so as to be as little as my master, to be with Him, to walk behind Him, step by step, as a faithful servant.'[14] Charles de Foucauld lived life with extraordinary generosity of spirit. He had a passion for living alongside the poorest in our world. He found fulfilment and total self-surrender and trust in God even in the face of failure.

Three aspects of Brother Charles' life are sources of encouragement for us today in these times of trial. First was his commitment to finding 'Nazareth' – the hidden place of encounter with God. After leaving the army, and while discerning a call to become a Trappist monk, Charles rather reluctantly followed the recommendation of his spiritual director Father Huvelin, who suggested he go to the Holy Land. For two years he stayed in Nazareth living in a hut on the grounds of the Poor Clare Sisters. This experience was a turning point in his life. It was in Nazareth that Charles discovered that it was in going down that he could be raised up to God. He writes: 'How clearly Jesus preached humility at Nazareth, by spending

---

13 Little Sister Kathleen, *The Universal Brother Charles de Foucauld Speaks to Us Today* (New York: New City Press, 2019), loc. 831.
14 Little Sister Kathleen, *The Universal Brother*, loc. 836.

30 years in obscure labours ... I must imitate the hidden life of the poor and humble workman of Nazareth.'[15] While Charles fell in love with Nazareth itself, he also came to realize that God was calling him to discover his own Nazareth – his own hidden and obscure place living alongside and serving the forgotten peoples of the Saharan desert.

'Nazareth is a house,' writes Father Huvelin to Charles, 'that you build in your heart, or better still, it's a house that you allow the hands of Jesus, the child so meek and humble of heart, to build inside of you.'[16] That place can be like a desert place:

> To receive the grace of God you must go to a desert place and stay a while. There you can be emptied and unburdened of everything that does not pertain to God. There the house of our soul is swept clean to make room for God alone to dwell ... We need this silence, this absence of every creature, so that God can build a hermitage within us.[17]

I wonder where your Nazareth place is in your life – where is the ordinary obscure place that Jesus is calling you to remain in and to seek: not prestige and recognition, but the company of those in the lowest place. For it is in humility that we are raised to God.

Second was his mission of friendship in the desert as a universal brother. Charles modelled a ministry of presence in exemplary ways. For him, adoration of the blessed sacrament and his ministry of friendship and kindness to the men and women of the Sahara were inseparable. His approach was to dwell with and learn from his Muslim neighbours, while at the same time living fully as a Christian, incarnating, insofar as it was possible, Jesus among them. The work Charles set out to do was marked by 'the suffering of love'. He built a small hermitage, hoping for brothers to join him, but no one was

---

15 Little Sister Kathleen, *The Universal Brother*, loc. 831.

16 Little Sister Kathleen, *The Universal Brother*, loc. 1075.

17 See www.spiritualityandpractice.com/quotes/quotations/view/12 740/spiritual-quotation, accessed 14.2.2021.

sent to him from the wider church. Instead locals visited him day after day – the poor, the lame, the lonely. He loved everyone who came to him and he was loved because he lived with them. Charles writes:

> I think there is no saying in the gospel that made a deeper impression on me and more transformed my life than this one: 'Whatever you did to one of the least of these you did it to me'.[18] There is a deep joy in all of this – a mission of friendship, where God's grace is reciprocated.

How much the Church of today can rediscover when it crosses the institutional threshold and goes out to meet women and men of all creeds and none. What friendships are waiting to be born in unexpected places!

Third was the abandonment to God as an interior compass. Charles' enduring perseverance was astonishing. His efforts were enormous, yet these appeared to yield very little fruit. Once Charles realized that the transformations he longed for would not come through greater effort on his part, he discovered the fruit of abandonment; of letting go. Abandonment is an attitude that recognizes God is always present to us, yet so often we operate out of our own efforts and forget to be present to God. Charles gradually came to identify with Jesus' own efforts, which conferred on them a new kind of fruitfulness – choosing poverty, utter lowliness, humiliation, rejection, persecution and suffering. Out of this abandonment to the divine sprang his most famous prayer. This is the only prayer I have ever memorized by heart. It is a prayer I have recited in times of uncertainty and darkness, and in times of fruitfulness and joy. But it is a prayer that cannot be taken lightly. When you pray it you are risking all.

Father,
I abandon myself into your hands; do with me what you will.
Whatever you may do, I thank you:
I am ready for all, I accept all.

---

18 Little Sister Kathleen, *The Universal Brother*, loc. 695.

Let only your will be done in me, and in all your creatures.
I wish no more than this, O Lord.
Into your hands I commend my soul;
I offer it to you
with all the love of my heart,
for I love you, Lord,
and so need to give myself,
to surrender myself into your hands,
without reserve,
and with boundless confidence,
for you are my Father.[19]

Before his death, Charles had written, 'I wish to be buried where I die, a simple burial, no coffin, very simple grave, no monument, just a wooden cros.'[20] At the time, Charles de Foucauld's death went largely unnoticed. Yet his imitation of Jesus' life in Nazareth was to make him one of the most influential church figures of the twentieth century, inspiring 21 congregations today. Charles' grave bears the inscription: 'I want to cry the gospel with my whole life.'[21] And this he did.

We might not all be called to the harshness and heat of the Saharan desert, and we might wonder where we discover our Nazareth, our hidden place with God; where in quiet faithfulness we can seek to imitate the life of Jesus, opening our eyes to the invitation to love and befriend those who take the lowest place at the table.

Pope Francis' latest encyclical, *Fratelli Tutti*, ends with these words:

I would like to conclude by mentioning another person of deep faith who, drawing upon his intense experience of God, made a journey of transformation towards feeling a brother to all. I am speaking of Blessed Charles de Foucauld. Blessed Charles directed his ideal of total surrender to God towards an identification with the poor, abandoned in the depths of

---

19 Little Sister Kathleen, *The Universal Brother*, loc. 2122.
20 Little Sister Kathleen, *The Universal Brother*, loc. 1819.
21 Little Sister Kathleen, *The Universal Brother*, loc. 252.

the African desert. In that setting, he expressed his desire to feel himself a brother to every human being and asked a friend to 'pray to God that I truly be the brother of all.' He wanted to be, in the end, 'the universal brother'. Yet only by identifying with the least did he come at last to be the brother of all. May God inspire that dream in each one of us. Amen.[22]

Carlo Carretto

There are certain books that you treasure all your life and always carry with you. One of those books for me is Carlo Carretto's *Letters from the Desert*.[23] It has continued to be a guide to me through this time of the pandemic.

The call. Carretto writes that God's call is mysterious: it comes in the darkness of faith. It is so fine, so subtle, that it is only with the deepest silence within us that we can hear it. And yet nothing is so decisive and overpowering for anyone on this earth: nothing surer or stronger. This call is uninterrupted: God is always calling us. But there are distinctive moments. I wonder if you have ever heard God's call. I wonder how that call came. I wonder how you responded.

Until you are capable of an act of perfect love. Setting out into the Saharan desert, in a jeep with two blankets, Carretto notices an old man shivering in the market town. He contemplates giving one of his blankets to him, but he does not stop. He thinks he may need both blankets to keep himself warm that night. In the middle of the night he wakes to see a picture in his mind of the old man shivering. What is worse is that he himself has not used the second blanket. He knows, despite his two blankets, he will never be warm again. Will he ever be capable of an act of perfect love?

---

22 Pope Francis. *Fratelli Tutti* (Associazione Amici del Papa, 2020), p. 212, paragraphs 286–7, Kindle edition.

23 Carlo Carretto, *Letters from the Desert* (London: Darton, Longman and Todd, 1972).

Solitude and prayer.[24] Carretto speaks of how in the desert you become attentive again to the things of God. Has this not also been our experience in these last months? His great joy of the Saharan novitiate is the solitude – silence, true silence, which penetrates everywhere and invades his being, speaking to the soul with wonderful new strength unknown to many. Carlo's words and stories, like Scripture, have a wisdom you carry with you through the desert or wilderness places of your life.

He comes to the realization that for many years he thought that everything depended on him. He writes that we were so busy in our action to save the world that we forgot that the weight of the world was on Christ's shoulders, not our own. As prayer becomes richer in content he discovers that it begins to use fewer words. Rather than petitioning or explaining, he seeks rather to make more room for God – using a prayer word, perhaps, like the echo of a wave breaking on the shore. He craves to remain alone, silent, motionless at the feet of Christ. 'I thought in prayer everything depended on me and my efforts, on the books passing through my hands and the beauty of the words and liturgy I used, but true prayer requires more silence than words, more adoration than study, more presence than rushing around.'

Purification of the spirit.[25] Carretto talks of the struggle through which we come closer to the God who seeks us. It is in disaster, boredom, depression, experience of failure and sin, sickness, loss, that we begin to discover what we really are – poor, fragile, weak and mortal. God's impenetrable night wraps around us bringing a terrible loneliness and abandonment. And in this deeply painful state prayer becomes true. The soul speaks to its God out of poverty and pain. Deep down the soul has understood that it must let itself be carried. What matters is to let God get on with it. How true this has been for me, and I believe for so many of us.

Contemplation on the streets. Charles de Foucauld wrote, 'If the contemplative life were possible only behind convent

---

24 Carretto, *Letters from the Desert*, chapters 5–8.
25 Carretto, *Letters from the Desert*, chapter 9.

walls or in the silence of the desert, we should in fairness give a convent away to every poor person and a strip of desert to everyone working hard in a bustling city to earn a living.' He decided to live the contemplative life on the streets. I do not want a monastery that is too secure. I want to live the contemplative life along the streets.

If you cannot go to the desert you must make the desert in your life. Live the intimacy of God in the noise of the city. Poverty is not a case of having or not having money. Poverty is a beatitude: 'Blessed are the poor in spirit.' It is a way of being, thinking, loving. Poverty can be a freedom, a detachment, a lightness of being, a truthfulness, a freedom. It is also love.

The revolt against the good.[26] One of his letters from the desert that I have never forgotten is the one Carretto calls 'The revolt against the good'. He speaks of the ulcer of resentment that can grow within us, which is hard to escape. The experience of feeling we have carried the burden for too long, that our service has been unrecognized, that we have been overlooked, treated as nothing, sacrificed our lives but for what ... Each one of us at this point could add our own narratives of rejection. And then one terrible day the ulcer bursts and the poison that has built up inside of us comes pouring out – and sometimes that outpouring can threaten years of relationship and self-giving. 'I've had enough.' We have not been heard. We have not been understood. We have been the victim. And of course for each one of us there is truth in that. 'How can I really love my neighbour who repays me with indifference or even derision?'[27] It is at this point, Carretto says, that the gospel begins. The rule of justice, he writes, is not enough. It is good, it is true – but it is not complete. Something else is necessary. And then Christ comes. What Christ does is lead us beyond justice into the unconditional mercy of God. Unless we have met Christ on the cross and at the tomb we will never understand that. But once we have, we will begin to understand that God's love costs not less than everything.

---

26 Carretto, *Letters from the Desert*, chapter 15.
27 Carretto, *Letters from the Desert*, p. 123.

Wonderings

St Benedict – Matthew 7.21–27

- I wonder in this present crisis what the sand is.
- I wonder in the present crisis what the rock is.
- I wonder what this great fall means to you.
- I wonder how we can rise again.

Julian of Norwich – Romans 8.26–end

- I wonder how God is your maker, keeper and lover.
- I wonder how God is with you in 'weal and woe'.
- I wonder if you believe all will be well.
- I wonder if there is anything that can separate us from the love of God.

St John of the Cross – Song of Solomon 2.8–17; 8.6

- I wonder which images from the Song of Songs speak to you.
- I wonder where God as the 'living flame of love' is at work in our world today.

Charles de Foucauld – Luke 14.7–14

- I wonder where your 'Nazareth' place is.
- I wonder what having a vocation to the 'lowest place' looks like for you.
- I wonder how the prayer of abandonment speaks to you.

Carlo Carretto's Letters from the Desert – John 6.35–40

- I wonder what Jesus means when he says he is the Bread of Life.
- Carlo Carretto talks about taking the last place at the table. I wonder what that last place feels like for you.
- I wonder what we can learn from simplicity and powerlessness.

10

Recentring Disability

FIONA MACMILLAN

At the start of 2020, disability work at St Martin's was flourishing. Over the previous six months we had celebrated our Disability Advisory Group's fifth birthday, finished a groundbreaking access audit of our sensory and physical environment, published a booklet to share our ideas with the wider Church, and held a pioneering conference on neurodiversity and faith. After nine years' work, there was a new momentum, a sense of things opening up – until lockdown.

St Martin's focus on disability experience began in 2011 as part of our commitment to draw in people often excluded from church and society. We seek both to work within our own community and to share our learning and resources with the wider Church. Within St Martin's the Disability Advisory Group lead us, and we work in partnership with Inclusive Church to hold an annual conference on disability and church. Together our work has flourished.

This work began in the shadow of austerity, against a backdrop of cuts to services and support that left disabled people particularly vulnerable.[1] The current pandemic has highlighted many of the gaps in society's safety net: the risks disabled people are facing from both the coronavirus itself[2] and the measures

---

1 F. Ryan, *Crippled: Austerity and the Demonization of Disabled People* (London: Verso Books, 2019).

2 C. Putz and D. Ainslie, 'Coronavirus (COVID-19) related deaths by disability status, England and Wales: 2 March to 14 July 2020', *Office for National Statistics*, 18 September 2020, available from www.ons.gov. uk/peoplepopulationandcommunity/birthsdeathsandmarriages/deaths/ articles/coronaviruscovid19relateddeathsbydisabilitystatusenglandand wales/2marchto14july2020, accessed 29.9.2020.

taken to contain it.[3] With these additional barriers to access and participation in community life, there is the additional risk that disabled people are subsumed as 'the vulnerable'[4] and, in a society measuring merit by income, less valuable.

But it is precisely this practice of vulnerability that could enrich society and particularly the Church. Many disabled people have long experience of being unable to access buildings and of building online communities; of reluctantly finding new ways of doing things because the old ways are no longer possible; of suddenly being confined to a space by limited capacity, pain or resources – and of learning to stay still and go deeper. These paradoxical gifts are being overlooked as society and church now colonize the spaces where disabled people dwell, and longed-for adjustments in work and worship are miraculously possible.[5]

The closure of church buildings during national lockdown has led to a flourishing of online worship, from livestreamed services to Zoom Lectio Divina. There is no 'one size fits all' – just as the church building is inaccessible for some, so online worship excludes for reasons from technology to resources to health. But it has also included some disabled and chronically ill people, who are now able to join regular worship and faith communities for the first time in many years. It has opened up conversations about the nature of online worship and of church itself, of practice that has long been present in disabled

3 Inclusion London, *Abandoned, Forgotten and Ignored: The impact of the coronavirus pandemic on Disabled people, Interim Report – June 2020* (Inclusion London, 2020). Available from www.inclusionlondon. org.uk/wp-content/uploads/2020/06/Abandoned-Forgotten-and-Ignored-Final-1.pdf, accessed 29.9.2020.

4 Office of the High Commissioner of Human Rights, 'Statement on COVID-19 and the human rights of persons with disabilities', Office of the High Commissioner of Human Rights, 9 June 2020, available from www.ohchr.org/EN/NewsEvents/Pages/DisplayNews.aspx?News ID=25942, accessed 8.11.2020.

5 N. Lawson Jacobs, 'Disabled people say welcome to our world', *Church Times*, 1 May 2020, available from www.churchtimes.co.uk/ articles/2020/1-may/features/features/disabled-people-say-welcome-to-our-world, accessed 29.9.2020.

communities,[6] and that may well continue long after those who are able are safely gathered again.

Within St Martin's disabled community some are now able to connect online across barriers of geography and experience, opening new conversations and growing community. Others are increasingly isolated and have heavy burdens to bear. We long for touch, presence and communion, and learn to be present to one another in new ways, valuing the small, the vulnerable, the ordinary. Yet while we are separated and waiting, still life grows in unexpected ways. The late Professor John Hull suggested that disabled people may have a distinct prophetic ministry to the Church.[7] Perhaps we were made for such a time as this.[8]

Disability Advisory Group

The Disability Advisory Group (DAG) brings together people with experience of physical, sensory, cognitive or mental health conditions or neurodiversity, either from our own lives or from living alongside others in our caring or work role. Open meetings once a term explore issues and ideas – both barriers to belonging and the insights that grow from living vulnerably. We share our learning and resources with the St Martin's congregation and community in a variety of ways.

The pandemic has brought particular challenges because the way we work is key to what we are able to do. Many of our members are among the more vulnerable to coronavirus and more likely to face significant barriers to both access and participation. Early in lockdown we began finding ways to stay connected. We contacted members to find out how they would prefer to stay in touch, and developed routines of emails, text, phone calls and post, including printing out group emails and posting them.

---

6 D. A. Thompson, *The Virtual Body of Christ in a Suffering World* (Nashville, TN: Abingdon Press, 2016).

7 J. M. Hull, *Disability – The Inclusive Church Resource* (London: Darton, Longman and Todd, 2014), p. 97.

8 Esther 4.14.

In June we had our first DAG meeting on Zoom. It was a steep learning curve as it was a first Zoom experience for many. We prepared and sent out a guide to Zoom and a member of the congregation offered to act as mentor. DAG members joined via landline phone, mobile phone, tablet or laptop. One could see but not be seen; another could hear but not see; some with sound sensitivity needed microphones to be muted to improve sound quality, others had dialled in and could only hear, so felt disabled if muted. People came and went throughout as we found ways to be together, recognizing and holding our competing needs because being together felt both fragile and important.

We shared experience and ideas. Of church in lockdown, what's good and what we are missing; of the pain of being misunderstood online, being blamed by a stranger for not being grateful when not able to hear the service.[9] Of the difficult things about daily lockdown life and what we have enjoyed – mainly the silence and the wildlife. And our painful experience of the wider world during pandemic as disabled people, blamed for not fitting into spaces and systems newly made by and for the well. Where we had identified barriers in online church we suggested solutions. Those who are affected by an issue often know what will work better. It's often simple things that make belonging or participation more possible. We are flagging and disconnecting and we get plenty wrong. But we will continue to navigate these new spaces by asking old questions: 'What's working well? What's not working well? What else could we do?'

Liturgy writing workshop

For some years it has been our custom to write new liturgy for our main Sunday Eucharist as part of the disability conference weekend.[10] It's a way of sharing the conference ideas with our

---

9 H. Campbell, 'Congregation of the disembodied' in *Virtual Morality*, edited by M. Wolf (London: Peter Lang Publishing, 2003), pp. 179–99.

10 F. MacMillan, 'St Luke's Day' in *Liturgy on the Edge*, edited by Samuel Wells (Norwich: Canterbury Press, 2018), pp. 111–21.

wider congregation and of sharing our church life with those who come for the conference. Initially this was a Eucharist and healing service for St Luke's Day, but more recently we have separated out the themes of disability and healing to the Sundays either side of St Luke's Day. The DAG host an hour's liturgy writing workshop and invite members of the wider congregation to join us.

We opted to work online so that those who were shielding could participate, and to invite in-person contributions from those without online access. We held an initial planning meeting via Zoom, selecting lectionary readings that worked best with the conference theme. We planned the workshop to be on Zoom with facilitated breakout groups and identified facilitators who were comfortable with the technology and had experience of writing liturgy to encourage participation. The workshop was advertised internally in advance to the DAG, and via the congregational Facebook group and weekly newsletter (email and post). It was advertised publicly on the day in the notices at the end of the main service and in the chat on the Facebook livestream. This enabled us to draw participation from regulars and also to welcome visitors who had joined us for the service.

We emailed round a worksheet with the readings and an outline of the writing tasks to everyone who had signed up. The workshop was scheduled shortly after the service, so those who had been present in church were appropriately spaced in the parish rooms while others joined from home. After a brief introduction we moved into breakout groups to work on the Confession and Fraction, Intercessions, Eucharistic Prayer, or Thanksgiving and Invitation. A DAG member was also invited to write a poem to read at the end of the service. Contributions were sent in by email over the next four weeks and lightly woven together. Hymns and choral music were chosen to fit with the conference theme. Readings and prayers were led by members of the DAG and the conference planning team, with some people present in the building and others pre-recorded from home.

Windows on the World

About two months into the national lockdown a DAG member asked for a picture of the bird-feeders in my garden. 'I wonder what other people are looking at every day, what they see out of their windows.' The sense of feeling stuck where we are and wanting to see each other's views led to creative connections. Jonathan Evens had a long-running series of photographs on his blog, Windows on the World, sharing both a window frame and what can be seen through it. But what if, as well as seeing each other's views, we could understand something of each other's perspective or life experience? What does the world look like from a wheelchair or if you spend most of your life lying down; if you hear voices, live with anxiety or with increasing visual impairment? We invited DAG members to share their 'window on the world' as a drawing, painting, photograph, poem or in prose. These responses became the first works in an online exhibition and brought art into the heart of our conference.

Telling Encounters: Windows on the World was an art workshop held on Zoom a month before our annual disability conference. Those who attended watched a presentation of the idea, followed by the initial gallery, then responded by making or writing their own work. The event ended with people sharing their work with the group, before sending it in for inclusion in the conference gallery. The workshop was repeated during the conference, each piece in the gallery growing insight and encouraging others to respond with their own work. The gallery will be shared online via the Inclusive Church and HeartEdge websites, with a second version that has an audio description. We hope the gallery will continue to grow understanding.

Telling Encounters: stories of disability, faith, church and God

Since 2012 we have worked in partnership with Inclusive Church to hold an annual conference on disability and church. Centred on lived experience, underpinned by theology, it is planned by and for disabled and neurodivergent people as a space to resource each other and the church. We had envisaged planning a simple ninth annual conference while looking ahead to our tenth anniversary year.

Conference planning meetings were moved online in mid-March as the majority of our disabled and neurodivergent members were anxious about coming into London. Our initial planning meeting was the first week of lockdown and a first substantive Zoom meeting for most. We took time to check in with each other before exploring possible themes, ideas and ways of working together during lockdown, agreeing some working partnerships and areas of interest.

In May we decided to plan for an online conference in October because, like us, the majority of our speakers and delegates would not be at public gatherings for the foreseeable future. We partnered with HeartEdge as our online hosts, working with St Martin's and Inclusive Church to hold the framework of the day. We were keen to reimagine the conference as an online event while retaining important aspects – a space for disabled people to gather, a time to resource each other and the church, and a strong participatory ethos. We were also mindful that being online would broaden our reach beyond those able to travel to central London. This brought both opportunity and responsibility to share our platform, draw in new experience, and be accessible to as broad a range of disabled and neurodivergent people as possible.

We decided to keep our particular combination of plenary talks, small groups, workshops and closing liturgy, and find ways to add something of our 'parallel' activities of art, a silent space and a marketplace. Teams worked on access, social media, logistics and content. Online platforms were chosen on the basis of accessibility: Zoom in meeting mode for the main conference space, backed up by a private Facebook group as a marketplace, a space for connecting and for streaming additional content.

To enable time for creative content to be developed in new ways we held two advance workshops, for art and music. A Path through the Woods was an experimental workshop devised and led by June Boyce-Tillman and colleagues from the University of Winchester exploring how to express pandemic experience through sounds. These were then woven into a piece of music in rondo form, in the style of Mussorgsky's *Pictures from an Exhibition*. The finished piece was premiered at the conference in a workshop which also shared the development, process and learning.

We had a steep learning curve to understand online platforms and accessibility. Where possible we identified disabled-led organizations modelling good practice and either replicated it or asked for their advice. Accessibility was our key priority for funding: we were able to arrange for both closed captions and BSL thanks to a generous offer to underwrite our access costs. We wrote up our learning into access guides for the conference, Zoom and Facebook, which are being shared more widely.

We decided on a maximum of 120 spaces, to enable a sense of gathering and building a community for the day. We set different ticket types: 60 per cent were earmarked for disabled or neurodivergent people, the remainder for family/supporters or professional/other interest. This also enabled us to balance experience in breakout groups. We provided information about the conference cost and asked people to pay what they could afford. We published basic access information with email and phone contact details to sign up for BSL or captions or to request other adjustments. Detailed access information covering the conference, Zoom and Facebook was emailed with the conference pack a week before the conference.

Plenary sessions were a mix of live and pre-recorded with BSL and captions available on request. We had a varied programme, mixing input and participation, and with good breaks to enable pacing. All plenary sessions were recorded and were available to catch up afterwards, so delegates were encouraged to take breaks as they needed. In the morning, facilitated breakout groups provided space to share experience; in the afternoon, topic-specific workshops ran as breakout groups; each had BSL in one and live captions in another. We closed with a liturgy led in BSL with voice translation.

The conference was supported by a wonderful staff team,

mainly drawn from previous delegates and the planning team. A briefing was sent by email followed by a Zoom staff meeting 48 hours before the conference – as a chance to pick up tech training and questions, and begin to build community. The meeting was recorded and sent to those who couldn't be there.

Our staff team included:

- Safeguarding lead: their name and contact details were posted in the chat at the beginning of each session.
- Chaplaincy team: available during the day for anyone who wanted to spend time talking, praying or being silent with a chaplain. Short descriptions of the chaplains and the process were included in the conference pack. Each chaplain had identified two 30-minute sessions in the day when they would be available. A chaplaincy coordinator held these details, matched need with availability, and hosted a separate Zoom chaplaincy space.
- Facilitators for breakout groups and workshops (these doubled up with other roles).
- Individual roles: Zoom hosting, answering questions, people-herding, technical lead, and a single host to compere, plus nine speakers/workshop leaders.

In the same way as the physical conference stretches the fabric and workings of St Martin's, so the online conference has stretched the learning and resources of HeartEdge – and us all. It is by far the most labour-intensive, complex event we have put on, with less time, fewer staff, all for the first time – and during a pandemic. It was a leap of faith.

The conference drew delegates from across the country, most of whom would never have come to London. Some were in ministry, others on the edges of churches and communities; several had not been to church for a long time, some were on their first Zoom call. Many began the day with their cameras off and ended with them on; most were still with us for the closing liturgy.

Around 20 gathered for a post-conference coffee time on Sunday on Zoom. We shared our responses to the conference, and to the morning service, where several had been moved to tears. For some this was their first time meeting with other disabled Christians; for others it was a first sense of church as a safe space. All were keen to stay connected and to meet again. Some are now joining the livestream midweek Eucharist and Zoom listening groups. We are wondering together about what might come next.

Shut in, shut out, shut up

During the pandemic many disabled people have connected online and developed support networks around the barriers, finding ways to encourage and resource each other. We have shared stories of growing discrimination, new barriers and reduced support. There's a strong sense that what's happening to disabled people isn't known, participation is harder and our voices are not heard. We are being overwhelmed, overlooked and silenced – or, shut in, shut out and shut up.

I spoke with friends and colleagues about this experience. We have all felt the need to call out about what is happening, what we know and what it feels like, to share something of our experience and ideas more widely. We had previously talked about the need for spaces where disabled people can talk to each other and share ideas with a wider audience, particularly in the church. HeartEdge offered us a platform to begin these conversations.

We set up a programme for three Friday afternoons in September and three in November. The speakers were all disabled or neurodivergent and we imagined the audience would be mostly non-disabled: perhaps 30 people on Zoom for 90 minutes, a mix of input and participation, and signposting to further resources. Beginning where we are – with Disabled People, Church and Coronavirus; then Neurodiversity; and finally Disability. In the second series we went a little deeper into the same subjects, exploring Post-pandemic Church; Neurodiversity and Intersectionality; and Social Justice and Church.

As it happened we drew 40–80 people to each event. A majority were disabled or neurodivergent people, at least half in some sort of ministry. People have joined from all denominations and from outside the Church; most were from across the UK, some from North America, Europe, Africa and India. The response has been overwhelmingly positive and hugely varied. For some it is new connection and the healing space of shared understanding; for others a new learning or a new call. Sessions were recorded and are shared via HeartEdge. We are learning as we go.

Resources

Susanna Wesley Foundation, *Podcast 2: Neurodiversity and disability in the church* [Podcast], 19 August 2020. Available at https://susanna wesleyfoundation.org/podcast-2-neurodiversity-and-disability-in-the-church, accessed 29.9.2020.

Inclusive Church, 'Disability Advisory Group: a model worth sharing' in *Something Worth Sharing* [Online], 2019. Available at www.inclu sive-church.org/sites/default/files/files/Something%20Worth%20 Sharing%20WEB.pdf, accessed 29.9.2020.

HeartEdge, 'Telling Encounters: Windows on the World' [Video file], 2020. Available at www.facebook.com/theHeartEdge/videos/telling-encounters-windows-on-the-world/3160407761525I5, accessed 29. 9.2020.

Inclusive Church, 'Disability conference', *Inclusive Church*. Available at www.inclusive-church.org/disability, accessed 29.9.2020.

HeartEdge, 'Shut In, Shut Out, Shut Up – Part 1 – Disabled People, Church & Coronavirus' [Video file], 2020. Available at www.facebook. com/theHeartEdge/videos/3128010727321634/, accessed 29.9.2020.

HeartEdge, 'Shut In, Shut Out, Shut Up – Part 2 – Neurodiversity & Church' [Video file], 2020. Available at www.facebook.com/the HeartEdge/videos/shut-in-shut-out-shut-up-part-2-neurodiversity-church/2690189714588158, accessed 29.9.2020.

HeartEdge, 'Shut In, Shut Out, Shut Up – Part 3 – Disability & Church' [Video file], 2020. Available at www.facebook.com/theHeartEdge/ videos/356095972197739/, accessed 1.11.2020.

HeartEdge, 'Shut In, Shut Out, Shut Up – Part 4 – Disabled People & Post-pandemic Church' [Video file], 2020. Available at www.face book.com/watch/?v=4519166184825394, accessed 27.2.2021.

HeartEdge, 'Shut In, Shut Out, Shut Up – Part 5 – Neurodiversity & Intersectionality' [Video file], 2020. Available at www.facebook. com/watch/?v=405906567204207, accessed 27.2.2021.

HeartEdge, 'Shut In, Shut Out, Shut Up – Part 6 – Disability, Social Justice & Church' [Video file], 2020. Available at www.facebook. com/watch/?v=131192265202436, accessed 27.2.2021.

I I

Reimagining Expatriate
Christian Identity

HARRY CHING

The word expatriate in the Chinese language is commonly
translated as 僑民 (*qiáo min* in Pinyin).[1] Overseas Chinese
nationals often use this terminology with pride, as the first
word *qiáo* represents a sense of prestige and sense of social
mobility, and *min* is simply the word 'people'. The right part
of *qiáo* is derived from the word 高 (*gao*) representing a great
height in a person's stature. The word expatriate was uninten-
tionally associated with me as I grew up and has continued in
my ministry as an Anglican priest since ordination. The Bishop
in Cyprus and the Gulf, Michael Lewis, once wrote in the
introduction of the diocesan website.

> The Diocese of Cyprus and the Gulf serves the people of ten
> different political jurisdictions. Our worshippers are of a
> wide range of nationalities. In Iraq, virtually all were born
> in the country and are citizens, but elsewhere we are mostly
> expatriates. Or should that be *migrant workers*? In popular
> usage there is something of a class, or at least an economic,
> distinction between those two terms. Yet every Nepalese
> or Pakistani labourer and Sri Lankan or Filipina maid is an
> expatriate with a proud personal and family history and a
> culture and heritage from another land; while very many
> who normally and quite correctly describe themselves as

---

1 See https://pedia.cloud.edu.tw/Entry/Detail/?title=%E5%83%91,
accessed 30.11.2020.

expatriates from Britain, America, South Africa, India and elsewhere are also in fact migrant workers: they have moved to this or that country from their own, to work. It is humbling that both rich and poor and middling, all migrant working expatriates, are to be found together in the majority of our congregations, along with those who have migrated in order to retire, in countries where that is permitted.[2]

In the pre-pandemic world, the international movement was fluid, and I was quite the living specimen. I was ordained deacon in Cyprus and priest in the United Arab Emirates. Very few ministers in the Anglican Communion have shared such a journey. After five years serving in an overseas international diocese, I found myself serving in the country where I was baptized and confirmed, as well as most culturally affiliated – Britain.

My working title at St Martin-in-the-Fields, Assistant Vicar for International Ministry, attempts to match the ever-increasing international dynamic of the church. After all, the biblical world has always been international; and often nomadic. Abraham migrated from Ur to Canaan, followed by Moses leading the Israelites out of Egypt; Jeremiah and Ezekiel prophesied in their time during the exile. The ministry of notable individuals often has unintended travel or adventure abroad. It is a privilege to have lived and served in numerous countries away from home, proclaiming the living gospel and supporting the life of the universal Church. The apostle Paul reminded his audience in his epistles that the God we worship is beyond borders. Apostles and missionaries have continued to evangelize beyond their comfort zones since Ascension Day. This chapter is not an autobiography, yet my own journey reflects the global perspective of the Church worldwide, encountering migration and its impact. I hope to continue to extend this vision during my time at St Martin-in-the-Fields; yet the coronavirus outbreak has cruelly crushed this aspiration indefinitely. The pandemic has changed how some of us imagine the conventional understanding of expatriate living abroad and the

2 See www.cypgulf.org, accessed 30.11.2020.

perception of churches associated with expatriate Christians. The Chinese congregation at St Martin's has also been heavily affected in the past months. I was licensed to my current role three weeks before lockdown. I barely had the chance to get to know all the staff within the organization or congregational members before the national lockdown began. How could one have a ministry to the international community without an incoming international community? My only such opportunity was anointing a young Norwegian visitor with holy oil after church on my second Sunday. It was not until the beginning of July that I was able to worship with strangers.

Home

My surname gives away my ethnic origin. But equally I can be taken for someone from Surrey over a telephone conversation for the first time. I first came to the UK for my secondary education and I have been legally British since birth. My native Hong Kong was never really that far away before the outbreak. In fact, it felt a lot closer as the years progressed, with the help of technology and affordable travel. The current pandemic has not only postponed various overseas weddings, ordinations and baptisms, it forces many of us to reimagine our own identity, faith and our interconnectivity with our loved ones overseas. The international movement of people has now become less fluid. How will this new norm challenge our interconnectivity as expatriate Christians with our home countries and in particular the future of the Anglican Communion, as we are all very proud of our global connection?

Christianity became a global religion when missionaries were aligned with imperial expansion. My native Hong Kong was the crown jewel which Britain found it hard to let go. Different denominations of Western Christianity expanded overseas and beyond Europe and the Middle East. Christianity was at its peak when Britain and other imperial powers conquered the rest of the world. Colonial chaplaincies were set up, overseas missionaries were established, and churches and cathedrals were built resembling those in the home countries of the imperial powers. There were plenty of overseas Anglican parishes consecrated across the British Empire as St George's or Christ Church. Even beyond the boundaries of the empire, Christ Church in Istanbul (formerly Constantinople) and St Alban's Tokyo are examples reminiscent of the little British Christian corners beyond the Commonwealth. I sometimes wonder if those worshipping at these Anglican churches overseas would share a comfort level with a diaspora Chinese person worshipping with us at our Cantonese and Mandarin services at St Martin-in-the-Fields.

St Martin's has also been a place of welcome to people of many different races and ethnicities. Those of West African and Caribbean heritage have become strongly integrated into the St Martin's community. Many remember hearing services from St Martin's on the BBC World Service when they were younger and brought affection for St Martin's with them as they came to Britain. Those who came to be part of the NHS and were based in central London often found its location and open-door character conducive to engagement. The support of St Martin's for the anti-apartheid campaign was also an incentive for some.

Just prior to lockdown we were fortunate to have the Revd Azariah France-Williams on placement at St Martin's, before he began his role developing a HeartEdge Hub church in Manchester. Azariah has recently published an influential book on institutional racism in the Church of England which also speaks into the experience of the Windrush generation within the UK and, as it was published shortly after the murder of George Floyd in the USA, into the international phenomenon of the Black Lives Matters protests. Azariah has begun discussion of the issues raised by his book here by contributing virtually to services at St Martin's, the HeartEdge Living God's Future Now programme, and by leading a discussion of his book and of BLM organized by our Global Neighbours Committee and Justice, Peace and the Integrity of Creation group. There is much more to do and discuss, yet our relationship with Azariah has enabled an informed beginning.

Away

Expatriates are the backbone of parishes in overseas Anglican dioceses such as in Europe and Cyprus and the Gulf. They rely heavily on individuals starting a new life overseas either to work or to retire. Very few parishes would have parishioners who have been worshipping there for decades or generations. There have always been big turnarounds of members each September and June. The coronavirus outbreak has changed the pattern of these movements and has jeopardized these parishes' survival.

My time serving the expatriate churches in the Gulf embraces our interconnectivity as expatriate Christians. Expatriate parents bring their children to churches of different denominations to baptize and worship and remind them of their cultural identity. Due to the limited number of church buildings in Muslim majority countries, occasional offices are often oversubscribed. It is also an eye-opening experience to encounter mixed couples from different parts of the world inviting families flying from diverse locations to participate in a baptism service. At weddings, bride and groom read out marriage vows in different languages from each other, promising to be faithful to one another for the rest of their lives. At these overseas expatriate churches, the openness of Anglicanism abides. During the pandemic much has departed from this norm, and I am eager to find out the impact on the future of these churches.

Since March 2020, most of us have not travelled internationally, or even domestically, and many expatriate 'swallows' have left their host countries and returned home. Members of both Cantonese and Mandarin congregations at St Martin's are currently worshipping with us online during dinner hours in the Far East.

My mother tongue is Cantonese, yet I barely used the language in my public ministry prior to coming to St Martin's. In fact, the very first time I presided over a Eucharist in Cantonese or Mandarin was in the St Martin's sanctuary. My first lunchtime Eucharist was held online and alone at home, a challenge to my own theological conviction that priests should not celebrate the Eucharist on their own; yet leading worship exclusively online for three consecutive months yielded a completely different perspective.

As a multilingual person I often ponder the linguistic boundaries in our Christian faith. Exchanging peace by handshakes symbolizes a great bond of Christian unity beyond our language barriers; likewise Holy Communion transcends languages. Whether the celebrant leads the Eucharist in Latin, Chinese or English, the sacrament remains available to all, rich or poor, migrant or expatriate. Drinking from the same chalice represents the deep connection with our fellow Christians beyond our home parish; yet it is now paused indefinitely. Social distancing has challenged the intimate connection of congregational practice and traditions of the Church for centuries.

Geography and expatriates then

The proximity of St Martin's to London's Chinatown inevitably gives it good reason to minister to the Chinese community in London and beyond. Prior to the coronavirus outbreak, commuters and visitors passed through St Martin's without noticing. There were many other reasons to visit the West End or Trafalgar Square.

St Martin's has been the link church between Hong Kong and British Anglicans for many years. Anglican Hong Kongers who came to study or work in the UK would often make a stop at St Martin's to introduce themselves. The establishment of the Mandarin-speaking congregation in the early 2000s has been a recent development to support the lives of many Mandarin speakers who are new to the UK. One of the main areas of pastoral care with the Chinese congregation has always been the support of overseas Chinese resettlement.

It was never my ambition to live an expatriate life. I was rather unwilling. As fellow expatriates might understand, it is never easy to be away from home, in particular away from a supporting network in times of crisis. In the first few weeks of lockdown, London felt like a foreign country, or a scene from the film *28 Days Later*. Working from 'home' alone, I reflected on my previous relocations. One of the main reasons I had not had trouble settling into life in Cyprus was because of its shared colonial history with my native Hong Kong. It was another island with great maritime advantage and it was not too difficult to chase the British legacy, buildings and garrisons, as well as local Cypriots who spent similar periods of time in the UK.

While there might be migrant workers who would proudly refer to themselves as expatriates, there seems to be a third group, the exiled Chinese community at St Martin's. With the pause on frequent international travels, suddenly I have become an exiled priest to an exiled community. In various visits to the elderly members of the Chinese congregation of St Martin's, I often ask them why they did not consider going back to Hong Kong to enjoy retirement. It transpires that for many Chinese settlers in the UK from the previous generation Hong Kong was very much a stepping stone for those fleeing China (like some Greek- or Turkish-speaking Cypriots who were displaced during the conflict in the 1960s and 1970s and subsequently came to the UK). Their cultural attachments to the UK seem relatively weak, yet they have probably spent more time in the UK than in their home countries. They remain culturally attached to the Far East, and often face linguistic barriers, and so became extremely vulnerable when access to the St Martin's church building was denied during the pandemic. Worshipping at St Martin's was vital to their spiritual well-being; something that online worship cannot replace.

The Chinese congregation of St Martin-in-the-Fields has been meeting in the church building for over 50 years. The Ho Ming Wah[3] Social Centre supports the members of the Chinese diaspora beyond our regular worshipping community. Bishop Ronald O. Hall's decision to ordain the first woman priest in the Anglican Communion, Florence Li in Hong Kong in 1944, was not his only legacy: he played an important role in building Hong Kong to become the metropolis of today.

---

3 Ho Ming Wah 何明華 was the sinolized name of Bishop Ronald Owen Hall, Bishop of Hong Kong, 1932–66.

Two pioneering Hong Kong women priests have had connections with St Martin's. The Revd Florence Li was ordained to the priesthood in a time of crisis during the Second World War; her priesthood inspired many Christians of both genders. Her bravery, at a time when women presiding at the Eucharist were not universally welcomed, is notable. There is a plaque dedicated in her memory in the south-west entrance of the church, as well as an icon of her presiding at the Eucharist in the Dick Sheppard Chapel. Many remember Florence's ordination as a monumental milestone in the history of women in the Church, yet her ministry in mainland China during the Cultural Revolution was equally inspirational.

The Revd Joyce Bennet was an associate minister of the parish for many years. Many of the existing members of the St Martin's congregation remember her well. She was very much loved and respected by all people. The older members of the Cantonese congregation share many legendary tales of her ministry. I was privileged to meet her in my early years as an ordinand. Long before her ordination she was known as an experienced educator, building schools and improving the livelihood of many people in post-war Hong Kong as a member of the city's Legislative Council. She was sent by the Church Mission Society in the UK to support the lives of others abroad. Bishop Hall, Florence and Joyce's legacies live on, and often people have forgotten that they ministered to people overseas for the majority of their ministries. The fact that both Joyce and Florence were expatriate priests has often been neglected; they were called to serve the most vulnerable people in need in desperate times.

Geography and expatriates now?

There is a Chinese idiom 衣食住行 (*yī shí zhù xíng* in Pinyin; literally the words for clothes, food, shelter and travel), commonly translated into English as 'basic essentials'. The pandemic has stripped many expatriates of their pride in living abroad and the privilege of frequent travel, and made them aware of their limitations and how fortunate they once were to be living with such extensive mobility. The pandemic has certainly diminished the pride expatriate Christians take in the Chinese word *qiáo*. Many members of the Mandarin congregation were 'swallows' before the outbreak, splitting their time between the Far East and Britain, making a living out of international trade or the movement of people. A significant number have left the UK to remain in China or elsewhere and face the prospect of not returning at all. With the Great FireWall of China, not all members of the congregation can share a social media platform with the rest of the congregation, making it extremely difficult to keep in touch. The pandemic has highlighted the cultural barriers between different parts of the Chinese community that were less visible when the congregation met physically. It is also worth noting that the difference in Chinese characters (simplified and traditional) was not an issue before the pandemic, as one could choose the preferred format of order of service when there was a combined service. It will take a monumental effort to make up the lost ground. We long for a day when Mandarin, Cantonese and English can be read out in the same service and hymns can be sung in different languages at the same tune.

St Martin's annual pilgrimage to Canterbury Cathedral was replaced in 2020 by a virtual alternative in May. St Martin's usually returns the favour in welcoming back a group of ordinands and priests in their early years of ministry hosted by the cathedral, visiting London in June. No such occasion took place this year. The group is usually filled with a good majority of young priests coming from the African provinces of the Anglican Communion, sponsored by the Anglican Communion and other relevant bodies. I was privileged to be part of this group one summer. It is a humbling experience to stay in touch with these clergy from other parts of the Communion and to be reminded of them in my own prayers. The trip to the Canterbury scholars' programme was, for many, their first trip away from home. Meanwhile those of us from the developed world have travelled, moved home, attending weddings, ordinations and baptisms overseas, by simply pressing a button to confirm our online bookings, without concerns about visa applications. The quarantine measures of international travel have brought us closer to them and reminded us of our limitations. We hope to welcome these scholars very soon.

The future

The pandemic has changed the perspective of expatriate Christians. The travel limitations reminded us of our home, our roots and our identity. We anticipate remaining separated from our overseas contacts in the near future. However, we are grateful for the bridges that have been built with fellow Christians from other parts of the world. Going back to the Chinese for expatriate, the 僑 (*qiáo*) in 僑民 (*qiáo min*) is often miswritten as 橋民 (*qiáo min*), which is understood as 'bridge people'. Our commission as expatriate Christians is to maintain these bridges and always be prepared to build more.

Like the Tokyo Olympics for athletes around the world, the Lambeth Conference was to have been the highlight of summer 2020 for many Anglicans: an occasion to remind us of a common identity as Anglican Christians by the gathering of bishops regardless of race, culture and language. It is now postponed until 2022 – 14 years since the last conference. We eagerly await this conference and hope that St Martin's will continue to play a significant role for Christians from all around the world, beyond the pandemic.

12

Praying Through Crisis

SAMUEL WELLS

This chapter perhaps gives the simplest journey through the first eight months of the pandemic of any in this book. At the start of the pandemic I wrote a special prayer because it seemed a momentous week. Thereafter, with only a couple of exceptions, it continued to feel like a momentous week, so I carried on writing a special prayer. These prayers speak for themselves; but may also speak in other times and places, just as poignant, and just as perplexing.

In the face of the virus (17 March)

God of searching and knowing,
your people Israel faced famine and wilderness,
and your church has known persecution and hardship.
Be close to all your children in this time of bewilderment and fear.
Make this time of cessation and isolation
one in which your Spirit reveals new ways to be together,
fresh discoveries in worship, different gestures of care,
and innovative forms of compassion.
Encourage the vulnerable, comfort the impoverished,
inspire the anxious and give wisdom to those who govern.
Lift up our hearts that we may see
the abundance of what is still beautiful and true,
not be captivated by what is lost and absent,
and find new gifts in ourselves and one another.
In the power of the Spirit and in union with Christ,
who knew what it meant to be alone. Amen.

As things get harder (20 March)

God of gentle presence,
you knew the ultimate separation
when on the cross Christ felt he was forsaken;
be with all who feel their Good Friday has come today.
Comfort those who have the virus.
Empower all who care for those in distress,
through medicine, acts of kindness or imaginative
    communication.
Be present to any who feel utterly alone,
without companion or health or hope.
Show us your face amid grief and bewilderment.
Inspire us to find new ways to be one with one another and
    with you.
And bring this time of trial to an end.
In Christ our Lord. Amen.

The long haul (3 April)

God of time and eternity,
in Jesus you warned us
to sit light to rumours and predictions;
free us from the need to know, to be right,
to second-guess, to be wiser than everyone else.
As in Christ you shared our earthly fragility,
be close to all who find solitude, confinement,
inactivity or lack of structure unendurable.
Send your Spirit on all who are desperately ill,
and on those who care for them.
Give patience and endurance to those who just want it all
    to end.
Prepare the hearts and lives
of those in countries yet to face up to the crisis,
and peoples who lack equipment and habits to address it fully.
Give us grace to find life in the particular,
find hope in the small blessings,

and find you in all things.
In Christ who faced hardship
that we might find eternal joy. Amen.

When we're supposed to be happy (10 April)

God of today and for ever,
at Easter you show us that love is stronger than death.
Inscribe in our lives glimpses of resurrection;
bring to the weary heart strains of zestful rejuvenation;
breathe into dry bones the limbering pulse of new beginning.
Teach us the discipline of joy,
that even when all around us seems dishevelled and discouraged,
your Spirit may lift our hearts as yeast enlivens dough.
In sure and certain hope that, whatever happens,
you will be with us always;
through Christ your Son our risen Lord. Amen.

To keep going (17 April)

God of life beyond death,
your risen Son breathed the Spirit of peace
upon fearful and discouraged disciples.
Through that same Spirit,
breathe courage and hope upon your people today.
Where your children face disease and danger,
give them strength and healing.
Where they endure hardship and poverty,
give them endurance and encouragement.
Where they encounter frustration and powerlessness,
give them patience and resilience.
Make this a time of discovery, depth and renewal,
in which we find the truth about ourselves, one another,
    and you.
And show us the face of the risen Christ, your Son, our Lord.
    Amen.

As acute emergency turns to chronic malaise (23 April)

God of now and for ever,
in Christ you promise you will be with us always,
even to the end of time.
Visit us by your Holy Spirit in this moment
when crisis threatens to become permanent.
Give patience to weary hearts, peace to troubled minds,
health to beleaguered souls.
Lay down in us habits of gentleness, perseverance and hope
that will sustain us long after the danger lifts.
Embrace us in our anxiety and meet us in our anger,
that in this time of exile we may see your Son's face like
    never before.
In whose name we pray. Amen.

On feeling small (1 May)

God of small things, in Jesus
you gave up always and became now,
you renounced everywhere and became here;
meet us in this season of fear, bewilderment and loss.
When our efforts seem tiny,
show us the thousands who care about what we care about;
when our skills seem insufficient,
reveal to us the many who seek the same goal.
Lift our gaze from what we miserably don't have
to what we wonderfully are,
that in joy and wonder at your glory
we may turn from emptiness and find fullness of life.
Through Christ in the power of your Spirit. Amen.

On easing of lockdown (15 May)

O God, the light of the minds that know you,
life of the souls that love you,
and strength of the hearts that serve you:
meet us when our minds seem stuck in confusion,
our souls stand lost in despair
and our hearts are plunged in desolation.
Give our hands good work to do,
that in serving the needs of others
we may rediscover ourselves while finding you.
Through Jesus Christ our Lord. Amen.

For the coming of the Holy Spirit (29 May)

God of rushing wind and tongues of fire,
in your Holy Spirit you turn the world upside down.
By the power of your Holy Spirit,
set our hearts on fire with joy and wonder.
Transform the sadness of many and the bewilderment of most
and make this virus season a time of renewal,
rediscovery, solidarity and discovery.
Show us your Son's face
in the face of the stranger, the hungry, and the lost,
that your Church on its birthday
may resemble its crucified and risen Lord.
In whose name we pray. Amen.

For lives that matter (7 June)

God of Abel and Cain, the one who was slain
and the one who denied complicity or responsibility:
visit those who can't breathe because of the virus
or because of oppression at the hands of another.
Raise up leaders who offer their people vision and hope;
empower any who dwell in the midst of violence

or live in the face of prejudice;
and make your people a rainbow
that promises plenty at the end of the storm.
In the name of Christ, our brown-skinned Lord,
in the power of the Spirit, who speaks in every tongue. Amen.

In bewildering times (14 June)

God of now and for ever, the far distant and the utterly intimate,
in Christ you told us not to try to guess the day nor the hour.
Fill our impatience
with compassion for those in a greater plight than we ourselves.
Replace our confusion
with clarity of understanding for what matters most.
Suffuse our self-pity for what we lack
with heartfelt gratitude for what you give us in abundance.
Heal our powerlessness, show us where best to employ
    our energies,
and humble us through the witness of those
from whom we expect little but who bless extravagantly.
In the power of the comforting Spirit
and in union with the suffering yet risen Christ. Amen.

For eagles' wings (19 June)

Everlasting God, you do not grow faint or weary;
your understanding is unsearchable:
yet your Son fell on the way of his sorrow,
and needed a stranger to carry his cross.
Look with mercy on those who live with exhaustion and
    bewilderment.
Renew their strength, that they may rise above
the powerless wait for news, guidelines and directives,
and, mounting up like eagles,
may find purpose, hope and fulfilment
in activity, in reflection, and in you:

so that despite discouragement and confusion,
they may run and not be weary, may walk and not faint.
In the power of your Spirit and in union with Christ. Amen.

For discovery in a garden (26 June)

God of seed and flower,
in the risen Christ you met Mary in a garden;
yet in the creation story we read
how we turn the garden of your abundance
into the prison of our scarcity.
Kneel with those who find themselves
in the Gethsemane of doubt, turmoil and fear.
Bless any who have known how that garden can change
into one of betrayal, flight and denial.
And lift our hearts to enjoy the garden of your glory,
where the leaves of the trees are for the healing of the nations.
In Christ and through the joy of your Spirit. Amen.

On feeling useless and helpless (3 July)

O God who, in Christ,
had arms swaddled in a manger
and hands nailed to a cross,
encourage any who feel their energy is being constrained,
their creativity held back, their goodwill going to waste.
Bless all who sense they are at the mercy of
events beyond their control,
decisions taken without their contribution,
developments about which they are the last to hear.
When our skills are overlooked and our role undermined,
give us patience and persistence, fortitude and forbearance,
respect and resilience, that in our bewilderment
we may grow in our understanding
of the power you express in weakness.
Through Christ and in the mystery of your Spirit. Amen.

In the face of hardship and fear (10 July)

God our strength and refuge,
you gather us like a mother hen with her chicks
and count each hair of our heads.
When we are convulsed by fear,
and worry that we'll lose things very precious to us,
walk with us, that we may find words for every anxiety
and companions amid our despair.
When we face hardship and adversity,
surround us with the abundance of creation, life and growth
that you give us for free.
Open our eyes to see others worse off than us,
joy springing up beyond us,
and love taking root around us,
that our small story be transcended by your wondrous glory.
May your kingdom come, your will be done.
In Christ and in the mystery of your Spirit. Amen.

For patience (24 July)

God of forever and a day,
your Son Jesus was urged by his disciples
to name the day and the hour.
Meet us in our urgency,
our need to know the future,
and our difficulty in staying in the present tense.
Walk with any for whom work and well-being and hope
depend on facts yet to emerge
and decisions that cannot yet be made.
Bless any who feel that time is ticking by
and certainty is further away than ever.
Visit your children who are overwhelmed with anxiety
and surrounded by unresolved challenges.
Make us a people who trust in your ways.
In Christ and through the Holy Spirit. Amen.

For those who can't see a way forward (31 July)

Merciful God, your children languished in slavery in Egypt,
your people endured exile in Babylon,
and your Son's disciples were devastated on the night of
    his crucifixion.
Be close to any who wake each day seeing no way through,
no hope emerging, no prospect for better times ahead.
Give them companions in their despair, patience to wait for
    your dawn,
and courage to endure till the light appears.
Show each one of us the wisdom of the past that can help us,
the experience of others that can enrich us,
and the pain of the downtrodden that can remind us
how many have things much worse.
Send on all your beloved creatures
the transforming gift of your Holy Spirit,
that we may know that nothing is impossible with you.
In Christ our risen Lord. Amen.

For those who feel trapped (9 August)

God of wonder and mystery,
your servants Joseph, and Daniel, and Peter and Paul
knew what it means to be in prison and to have nowhere
    to turn.
Be close to any who feel they have no idea what to do,
no plan how to make a living, no direction in which to travel,
no foundation of hope on which to build.
Bless all who feel trapped in their home, in a relationship,
in their work, or in a neighbourhood.
Send your Holy Spirit on those who feel incarcerated in their
    own body
or by the unpredictability of their mental health.
Show each one of us power we didn't know we had.
Visit us in companions that speak of your mercy.

And make us a point of release for another
whose existence is more challenging than our own.
In Christ our Lord, who left the tomb that we might live to
the full. Amen.

For endurance (16 August)

God of for ever and today,
in Jesus you took on a human life
in all its joy and despair, its weariness and intensity.
Walk today with all who wonder how they can find
patience in the midst of uncertainty,
hope in the context of bleakness,
and energy amid powerlessness.
By the power of your Holy Spirit,
show your children glimpses of your truth,
reminders of your faithfulness,
and rewards in the wilderness,
that we may discover in you
the strength and confidence we need to keep going
and the grace to encourage one another.
Through Christ your Son,
whose resurrection is our guiding light. Amen.

When things are bleak (4 September)

God of for ever, visit our hearts when hardship is very present,
good news seems scarce, and the future looks empty.
As you visited your children in the wilderness, your prophets
in prison,
and your Son's disciples in the upper room,
come among us now by the power of the Holy Spirit.
Bring us deeper friendships than we've ever known,
show us wisdom like never before,
and surround us with company
of those worse off than ourselves;

that we may find hope to carry on, and faith to live by,
in the love we discover in one another.
In Christ our Lord. Amen.

On losing something precious (11 September)

Ever-present God, your Son Jesus wept at the tomb of Lazarus
and your people Israel were lost in lament
as they left the ruins of Jerusalem and went into exile.
Be close to all who are losing their job, their livelihood,
their community, or their joy in life.
Make their endings ones of dignity,
their memories ones of pride,
and their legacy one of deeper faithfulness.
Meet each one of us in our places of grief and loss,
that as we perceive the agony of your Son's cross
we may discover the glory of his resurrection.
In Christ and through the power of the Spirit. Amen.

To find manna in the wilderness (18 September)

Providing God, you led your children through the wilderness
with pillar of fire and of smoke,
you made yourself known to your people in exile
as one who shared their suffering,
and you were with the disciples after the crucifixion
and again after the ascension;
give us manna in our wilderness.
Show us the truth that never fades, the glory that never falters,
the wonder that never diminishes.
Fill our eyes, our ears and our hearts
with the abundant life of your creation,
that even as our own lives are inhibited and constrained,
we may praise you for the dawn, the birdsong, and the joy of
    one another.
Free us from the fear that your love won't be enough for us.

And by your Spirit, empower us to walk with those
who suffer more than we do.
In Christ's name. Amen.

For those trying to learn and to teach (25 September)

God of wisdom and understanding, your Holy Spirit leads us
   into all truth.
Bless those trying to share knowledge and inspire all who are
   seeking to discover.
Give them grace to transcend the limitations and regulations
   of the pandemic.
Fill them with patience and discernment
as they arrange and follow guidelines and requirements.
Restore any for whom this season is one of despair,
   disillusionment or discouragement.
Shape the hearts of your people to live with uncertainty,
labour in spite of fragility, and find compassion for those at
   greater risk than ourselves.
Make this a time we look back on as one when we learned
   who we are, and who you are.
In Christ our risen Lord. Amen.

For those who feel alone (2 October)

God who is three and one, your Son was surrounded by people,
and chose disciples, yet was sometimes very alone.
By the power of your Holy Spirit, be a companion
to any who feel isolated, abandoned or forgotten.
Walk with those who nurse deep wounds,
all who struggle with profound fears,
and any who have no one with whom to share
   troubling secrets.
Teach each one of us to be our own friend,
in comfort and in challenge.
Embrace any who seek oblivion

because they can't face the burden of what they're going through.
And meet us in the places
where we struggle with pain, grief or regret.
In your Son Jesus Christ. Amen.

For those who can't plan (9 October)

God of now and forever,
your Son said we wouldn't know the day or the hour;
and yet we bind our lives by dates and projects, anticipation
    and plans.
Give your grace to all who feel they can set no expectations
or put any shape on the future.
By your Holy Spirit fill with patience
those who are exasperated with uncertainty
and long to know when things may return to normal.
Make us a people who dwell in your time and walk in step
    with you.
As you give us all the time we need,
embrace us with your eternal changelessness.
In Christ our Lord. Amen.

On entering tier 2 (16 October)

Intimate God, who in Father, Son and Holy Spirit
are utterly in and with one another and us:
dwell in the hearts of all who hear news
of more severe measures with trepidation and apprehension.
Give those who live with uncertainty
a deep sense of the closeness of your Spirit.
Uphold all whose livelihoods are jeopardized
and give them hope of better times to come.
Visit each one of us in the night-time of our worst fears.
And make this time of disruption one in which
we better come to know ourselves and you.
In Christ our Lord. Amen.

For those whose faith is fragile (23 October)

God of our every breath,
in Jesus you met one who said, 'I believe; help my unbelief.'
Meet all who whose confidence in themselves, others, or you
is like a fraying cloth or an unravelling spindle.
By the power of your Holy Spirit,
show the face of your Son to any who see
only hollow grief and empty darkness.
In the heat of our disappointments and the fire of our
    agonies,
be with us in silence, touch and words,
that even when we can't believe in you,
we may be overwhelmed with wonder that you believe in us.
In Christ our Lord. Amen.

On entering second lockdown (6 November)

God of mercy, in Christ you turned the grave
from a prison to the gate of life eternal.
By your Holy Spirit, give us grace
to turn the next season of quarantine
into time of renewal and growth;
to let the constraints and deprivations of these weeks
become causes for greater gratitude
for the blessings we generally share;
and to allow our sense of our own struggles
become an invitation to perceive
the greater challenges of others.
In him whose hands were nailed in agony,
and yet forgave and blessed as he died,
your Son, Jesus Christ. Amen.

On hearing of a vaccine (13 November)

God of healing and transformation,
in Christ you lay down your life
that we might find the safety of your kingdom.
Guide your people how to receive news of a vaccine for
     the virus.
As you look first to the most vulnerable,
direct the energies of public health officials
to those who need protection most,
and strengthen the hands of all who distribute and
     administer.
Make your Holy Spirit something we can never be
     inoculated against.
And keep us mindful of where our true salvation lies.
In Christ your Son our Lord. Amen.

On facing the fragility of life (20 November)

God of time and eternity,
in Jesus you entered the fragility of our earthly existence.
Walk with us as we witness the fragility of our own lives,
of democracy, of government, of public health,
of the economy, of so much we hold dear.
Show your people where to place their trust.
Give us wise leaders, resilient relationships and patient hearts.
Shape our society as one that upholds the vulnerable,
and your Church one that sees your Son's face in the
     stranger.
Lift up our hearts, that we may lift them up to you.
In Christ our Lord. Amen.

On entering Advent when we've really been in it a long time (27 November)

O God in whom the future is always bigger than the past,
raise our eyes to the things that are above,
that we never lose sight of your forever;
lower our gaze to the inevitability of our mortality,
that we may recall we are your creatures;
and direct our sight to those things in front of us,
that in the power of your Holy Spirit
we may face them with humility and hope,
knowing you were with us in Christ
and in him will be with us always. Amen.

During a very long Advent (6 December)

God of time and eternity,
when we strive to find you, you come towards us;
when you come towards us, you come as a baby;
when you come as a baby, you dwell in a manger.
Turn our eyes from the skies above
to see you in the humble earth before us;
when we see the humble earth,
turn our eyes from Herod's palace to the lowly stable;
in the stable, turn our eyes
from the good shepherds and wise kings to the helpless child.
And in the helpless child, reveal to us your glory. Amen.

13

Creating a Community of Practitioners

ANDY TURNER AND JONATHAN EVENS

It has been widely reported that Covid-19 and the impact of the virus has brought to the surface all manner of social inequality and opportunity, previously under-reported or hidden. The Church has seen something similar. Corners of the Church, including those busily getting on but sitting outside more vocal forums, have perhaps found a home – a place for ideas and support. Here pastors, ministers, clergy and volunteers, those overseeing smaller congregations, uneasy with forums, resource networks, new initiatives or time-wasting talk shops have found space for a renewal movement they didn't know they needed. Others passionate about people, community, issues of social justice, have encountered solidarity, empathy and support. Even those worn out by pandemic, weary of happenings beyond the local, have unexpectedly found HeartEdge – the movement launched in February 2017 by St Martin-in-the-Fields – to be something essential.

What is HeartEdge? A network, in part, for those who don't do networks; a forum to join in, for non-joiners everywhere. The movement aspires to be a community of hope, cultivating an understanding of mission reimagining church and society based around commerce, culture, compassion and congregational life – our four Cs. HeartEdge believes that congregations grow as they engage with the kingdom, that is, the sphere of the Holy Spirit's activity beyond the Church. This engagement comes in three specific forms:

- Compassion: partnering with others in forming relationships that release the gifts of strangers.
- Culture: making the church an estuary where creative energies are expressed and celebrated.
- Commerce: finding income streams to achieve financial sustainability and grow flourishing programmes.

Through HeartEdge, communities mentor one another, offer consultancy days to one another, and meet in larger gatherings to exchange ideas, encouragement and challenge. It seeks not to create clones of St Martin's, but to become the international embodiment of those committed to the vision to be 'At the heart. On the edge.'

With a small part-time team in London to provoke, mobilize and administrate activity far and wide, HeartEdge attracted interest from a breadth of different churches through word of mouth. If HeartEdge was a social movement, then it was one that emphasized the importance of networking and communication. With the onset of the pandemic in March 2020, a series of gatherings were promptly cancelled. What to do?

Zoom had not been on our horizon or in our vocabulary pre-lockdown. With hindsight that was a crazy place to be, although it was where most – although not all – of the church had also been, meaning that without the pandemic the explosion of virtual church would almost certainly not have occurred. The manner of this explosive growth means that there are currently many unanswered and unresolved issues, together with an enhanced level of creativity compared with what would have been seen should a longer and more measured development have occurred.

There have been three main phases to our embrace of the virtual within HeartEdge: getting online; developing a programme; and global connections. Within this process we prioritized, first, hearing the voices of those already online; and second, creating community.

In the first phase from March 2020 we were primarily reactive. Our modus operandi up to that point had been primarily relational; lots of people came to St Martin's from all around the world to see what we do and talk through how we do it, but mostly, in HeartEdge, we went to where others were. We had a roadshow introducing people to HeartEdge and our mission model – the four Cs. We would bring small teams of HeartEdge people to a church to listen and reflect for a day with the people of that parish. As HeartEdge grew, we were travelling further and for longer. At the beginning of 2020 we had already been in the USA, Netherlands and Belgium for HeartEdge events, as well as Edinburgh, Hamilton, Inverness, Portsmouth, Manchester, Milton Keynes, Norwich and Nottingham. HeartEdge is about ground-up initiatives that are context-based. We were clear it wasn't to be a London-centric movement, nor was it to be solely centred on St Martin's.

That all ended on 16 March, as did a whole series of events we had organized and were preparing to run. Those would have taken us to Amsterdam, Christchurch, Exeter, Liverpool, Penzance and Utrecht. That was our *raison d'être*, it was what had built the movement from its launch at St Stephen's, Walbrook in February 2017. What would we do now?

The answer to that question was Zoom; software about which we knew nothing and with which we had no experience. We had a network in HeartEdge and were part of others, so we tapped our networks for ideas and information before opening an account and beginning to use it. At first there were just three offerings. Lockdown was a new world; one that none of us really knew how to navigate. That reality revealed afresh what we already knew; that Scripture does not operate as an instruction manual providing a solution to any and every situation. Instead, Scripture shares a story that we enter and within which we improvise our part on the basis of what has gone before and the hints we have of how the story ends. With that in mind, we figured we, and others, would benefit from a regular opportunity to explore what improvisation might look like in the context of the pandemic. As improvisation evolves within the parameters of the story, we thought our exploration should happen through discussion; a central conversation that others could join and to which they could contribute. As a result, we created a monthly conversation that put Sam Wells in dialogue with theologians and practitioners while those joining them in the Zoom room responded in the chat to what they were hearing in ways that continued the discussion and, through questions, expanded the conversation. Sam's conversation partners have included Walter Brueggemann, John McKnight, Barbara Brown Taylor, Rachel Treweek, Chine McDonald, Stanley Hauerwas, Kelly Brown Douglas and Steve Chalke, and their conversations have ranged from community development and race to international aid and envy, while combining creativity and contemplation with protest and politics.

Our colleague Sally Hitchiner suggested that preachers would value an opportunity to explore how the lectionary readings could speak into the strange new world we were all inhabiting. In Sam Wells and Sally Hitchiner we had an ideal combination; two priests with substantial media experience, able to speak profoundly and accessibly about the Bible. The first week we filmed them sitting on the sofa in the vicarage flat as they chatted through the lectionary readings. From then onwards they were in a Zoom room with their conversation livestreamed to the HeartEdge Facebook page. It's a simple format that works because of the rapport between Sam and Sally combined with the depth of insight that they bring to the passages. Sam preached St Martin's through the early days of lockdown, opening up Scripture to reflect on stages of the pandemic and the stages of our personal reactions and responses. The Sermon Preparation workshops were where all the alternate sermons that he could have preached were shared, held up to the light and examined before being put back in their boxes. For him, at least; but not for those listening, who took away inspiration and ideas for crafting their own Sunday sermons.

Our third early offering was the Community of Practitioners. This had had one previous analogue outing. Catherine Duce had set up a practitioners group for London clergy which had met once as we anticipated that it would gather on a quarterly basis. A simple format for sharing was used – each person brought one recent experience, which was followed by a wondering in response shared by their neighbour and ending with the right to respond. The opportunity to reflect then passed to the neighbour and so on until the whole group had experienced both roles. Additionally, we built in opportunity for theological reflection with Sam via discussion of a chapter from one of his HeartEdge books. The format was readily adaptable to Zoom.

At this early point in our online development, we were experimenting with ideas and technology, learning from those things that didn't work as much as those that did. What was to push us into phase two of our development was the introduction of panel-based workshops that explored an aspect of the four Cs, particularly when it was an area in which the pandemic was making new demands and asking new questions of us. Growing Communities Online was a workshop series that began as a one-off workshop with Sally Hitchiner, Adrian Harris (from the Church of England's digital team) and Lorenzo Lebrija from our US partner, the experimental TryTank initiative. They shared stories of how churches were creating community online and caring for their congregations during the pandemic, including those unable to be online.

Initially we developed ideas and used contacts of the Heart-Edge team and wider St Martin's colleagues, but as we moved into phase two we began to do less ourselves and became more responsive to the riches within our movement. That shift was represented particularly by a series that Miranda Threlfall-Holmes prepared and presented on Difference, Diversity and Deviance. Miranda devised the format and found the guests to whom she talked. We provided the platform and a developed and branded programme within which it could sit. Our programme was now called Living God's Future Now, based on our understanding that the Church is called to anticipate heaven in the here and now; perhaps never more so than during a pandemic. In phase two we moved from delivering content to be consumed by our community to the kind of interactive exchange that characterizes HeartEdge at its best, with a recognition of the riches possessed by others in our community and the understanding that our role is to enable those riches to be shared by all our community.

Phase three has been to see these online community developments become our principal mode of operation, particularly in regard to those outside the UK. We are creating HeartEdge Hub churches within the UK able to share resources – their own and HeartEdge's – with others in their region or within their virtual specialism as, for example, a rural, coastal or suburban church. Increasingly, we are also seeing, outside the UK, the development of national HeartEdge Hub churches, sharing resources more widely with a nationally based community of HeartEdge churches. Our growing international contacts are increasingly enabling cross-cultural conversations which respond quickly and reflectively to major events such as Black Lives Matter and the US election. A recent partnership between the CEEP Network and HeartEdge has initiated a regular series of transatlantic conversations on topics such as the painful legacies that made the Black Lives Matter protests necessary, ways to vote on the basis of conscience and faith, plus living as agents of reconciliation in our increasingly divided societies.

Our experience in lockdown has been that the connections and networks that a movement like HeartEdge can provide have never been more needed. We have also found that connecting virtually through our ongoing programming and our support or practitioner groups offers the inspiration, ideas, networks and sounding boards that people need in such challenging times. One of our Community of Practitioners spoke about the impact of realizing that this is a global thing:

This is not a little group in London or little group in the UK. This is global. This is affecting people everywhere. And our struggles are very similar. We're all in different countries and it didn't matter how big our church is or isn't, whether we're in the city or in the rural areas; this is a global effect that is facing everyone. How do we, as human beings, without titles, without labels, how do we deal with this? Maybe in your context you have pastoral set-ups and support mechanisms, but for me this has been really genuine, simple, but beautiful and authentic.

HeartEdge emerged during a period of social and cultural change in the UK – from the dominance of social media to increased division. The 2008 global financial crash, the 2016 UK referendum on membership of the EU, and a series of elections all pointed to a fragmented society. Alongside this, the dominant narrative for churches remained doggedly one of declining numbers and a relentless focus on deficits – ageing congregations, lack of money and failing buildings. Some church leaders report a perceived increase in top-down managerialism and a focus on measurement – typically 'bums on seats'. As a consequence, some church leaders feel increasing anxiety, and an overwhelming feeling of inadequacy and failure. Add to this toxic brew a global pandemic, and it's possible to find isolated, locked-in and lonely church ministers overseeing congregations that no longer meet, alongside a mushrooming of complex social need on the doorstep, adding challenges to their care of souls. A regular at the HeartEdge practitioners group summarized the challenge:

It pretty quickly spiralled into the abyss, and I needed some help ...

I remember for the first three weeks, I sat at my desk after lockdown. Probably, sometimes from nine in the morning till nine at night, just almost glued here trying to work out how we were going to manage. And I remember saying, 'Will I have a church left at the end of this?' Because the way in which I minister, and the way in which we've operated, is very visual. So, when people gather I scan the room and I have an idea of what's going on and who's doing what. And then all of a sudden, everybody's disappeared. And yet I still somehow have some sort of responsibility for them and with them. And, you know, we have people with no technology. So, it was very consuming. Very, very, very consuming and very strange ...

Another referred to the shift online.

I think [the lockdown] was incredibly and totally overwhelming. And to be in church one Sunday and then realize that you were not going to be there and fumbling with Zoom and having some pretty failed attempts at trying to worship and trying to figure it all out.

Relationship and reality have been golden threads throughout the development of HeartEdge. In turbulent times, HeartEdge needed to be a vehicle that could enable people to join in, make useful connections, share their experience and find solidarity and support. HeartEdge also needed to promote an alternative way of being, in contrast to the dominant culture of anxiety. During the pandemic, a regular ongoing weekly practitioners' group became the possible forum to try this out – hosted by Sam Wells alongside a member of the HeartEdge team, and all undertaken on Zoom.

From the get-go the notion of an open group online that could also function as some kind of safe space to share insights and nurture support seemed unlikely. This may explain why the group started with a simple format – part book club, with the author along for the ride, and part reflection with everyone sharing a headline. No mention of 'safe space' and 'support'. Just the simplicity of Zoom and the opportunity to show up and contribute. It proved attractive. Speaking in August 2020 about the group, participants commented:

> It was lovely to come to something that somebody else had organized. I could just show up … that one huge gift, that I could just show up to something that was organized and be part of. And, yes, I mean from the book to reflection …

> What really got me was the honesty of some of the folks in this meeting about this desire for relevance.

The opportunity was open to all; one person said:

> I didn't think I was allowed … I'm not Anglican, I'm not British. I sort of thought, 'Why am I allowed to be here?'

The group would use a book as a focus for discussion – the obvious choice was the recently published HeartEdge manifesto and explainer *A Future that's Bigger than the Past*. Here Sam Wells as author theologian in residence and reflective practitioner joined each session. Each week Sam was available to provide the overview of the book's chapter, discuss practical implications and dialogue around questions as they came up – either 'in the chat', or by someone tuning in, switching on their mic, and sharing their question or comment directly. Following the 45-minute discussion the format morphed into reflection, using a format of sharing a headline of the week – with a colleague and, initially, a stranger on the call invited to respond with a wondering.

The encounter provoked by a disclosure proved challenging and also rewarding:

> ... a really good kind of pressure to engage with other people, because it would have been my tendency to just sort of sit back and take what I wanted, and then get out of there. So ... I just felt really trusted even though no one knew who I was.

> I was just really amazed at how quickly connection could be made with people who didn't know each other ... the nature of the way in which it was done was utterly terrifying. Yet, the second time round, you knew, this was a really special game ... And what it did was it created some really 'real' connection. Because there's no hiding. And if you didn't like it you just didn't turn up ... What it achieved was a connection ... some people here have said some really important things into my life. They don't really know me from the back of a bus, but there was that amazing connection that was really special.

> I'm an incredible introvert, so without those wonderings I probably never would have opened my mouth. And they really forced me and ... after the first couple of times I got comfortable with them. I no longer felt like I have to drink three cups of coffee before I can do it. But there was something about the group that made it safe, and said that, you know, I was part of it ...

Others agreed – the process of this special connection developed:

The wondering ... was really, really significant. In the beginning of feeling not alone in navigating this really uncertain time, now though the questions we might come up with were different from each other ...

The practitioners' group also had a key role in fronting up to the real changes in society and church the pandemic was exposing, and alongside this opportunities to rethink ways of being church.

What I really needed was a reflection on our role as a church, especially now. I desperately needed it and that's what the group was giving me ... I came for Sam, but I stayed for the group. I really needed that kind of mirroring and the reflection of others. I felt like, OK, this is an opportunity. But I was so isolated ... I do need that kind of direct engagement with people and to see how they're doing on a Sunday ...

This space to reflect on ways of being church in a changed world was important:

What does the shape of church look like? Having led something for nearly 30 years, and beginning to ask the question, 'I'm sure it can't be like this for ever?' You know, gathering in a building on a Sunday and all the different meetings that go on throughout the week, people were getting busier. It was incredibly more challenging to get. So, I was keen that before arriving in the practitioner group and then suddenly landing with this group, it was incredibly timely ... that these are questions other people were asking. I hugely appreciated the richness of what people were sharing from their own context.

Crucially the session was not a monologue. Lively dialogue developed as the group engaged and interacted, shared and contributed:

... the phrase that kept coming to me is just this embarrassment of riches ...

... so much church stuff, you sort of turn up as a consumer, you just kind of receive stuff. And if you try and participate, you're kind of told off really because you're meant to be the [one] receiving ... It was also the gift to be invited to participate and actually – we were all treated as adults, and as kind of valid contributing people, whatever state we showed up in, that was accepted ... it was welcomed and valued. And that's really rare.

Always enriching, always there were takeaways. You know there's always something that somebody had said, that you hadn't read, and you hadn't thought of. And that for me it was a lesson ... to trust God to be at work in that has been a real eye-opener. So – I'm really quite relaxed about [what] may or may not happen next.

Alongside finding support and ways forward was an opportunity to be 'real', 'authentic' rather than something else.

You made it feel really safe space to be real and authentic with whatever we were facing ... I didn't feel any embarrassment. Or shame in kind of turning up, feeling in a complete and utter mess. I don't feel any pressure to be shiny, or to try and portray a shiny story. Which is different from many church gatherings.

Social movements depend on simple networks and easy ways for communication. One unlikely and remaining outcome from the pandemic is a space for HeartEdge – for those at the heart or on the edge, to create and share online resources, and to meet regularly together and find support. That moment to talk theology and then share experience putting ideas to the test in the crucible of our own context and practice has proved to be a lifeline.

With thanks to Des Figueiredo, Edward Hopkins, Madeline Light, Rachel Noel, Chris Precious, Maryalice Sullivan and Nigel Wright.

14

Finding Faith at Home

SAMUEL WELLS AND SALLY HITCHINER

Before we look at how we can help people to find faith at home, we need to ask another question: 'How do you help people to find faith anywhere?' It sounds a simple enough question to answer. You get close to someone, you open your mouth, and you tell them about what you believe. Perhaps you deconstruct some of the obstacles they have to believing what you believe. It's a very flexible approach. It can happen through a book-group model or a dinner-party model, it can happen through an after-dinner speaker or a formula learned that can easily be drawn as a diagram on the back of a napkin in a pub. It sounds simple enough.

And yet, while there is a lot of good in those models, many Christians feel uneasy about them. We (Sam and Sally) wondered if there was another way of thinking about faith sharing. What if we started with the message we wanted to get across, and formed a model around that? We started with two central convictions: (1) that the Holy Spirit is already at work in each person's life from the day they are born or even before; and (2) that in any group gathered God gives us everything we need, to be Christ's friends and to be reconciled to each other, ourselves and the wider world – if we have the imagination to see it.

The first step was to use these two assertions to find people wanting to explore with us. If it really is true that God is already at work in the lives of everyone on the planet, then a certain proportion of people might be interested enough to come to our group. Tentatively Sally gave a notice at the end of one of our Christmas Eve carol services. 'In any group this size there will be a few people who would like to explore the Christian faith for the first time, or the first time after a significant break. If that's you, you're in luck; we have a new course starting in January. If this is you, find me at the end and give me your details.' Six people did. After the first week a couple of them brought friends. We had our first group.

We should explain how the group works in practice. We started the first group meeting in a room in the church. But with the first lockdown, we quickly moved online to Zoom, running subsequent courses entirely online. The group sizes are small: six to ten guests and two hosts. We get on to quite a deep level straight away, by asking each other a simple question: 'What's been at the heart of your week?' What this question does is not only to cut out the need for a long narrative of circumstantial detail, instead going straight to the jugular; it also focuses on the heart – the feelings, impressions and learnings – not just dispassionate events or curious coincidences. This question treats each person's week as a project, and thus lifts it out of the mundane and makes it worthy of other people's appreciative scrutiny. Already we have a sense of what's really moving in one another's lives.

All that doesn't take as long as you might think: with ten people, perhaps ten or 15 minutes. Then we come to the real work we do together. We call it the wonderings. We've adapted a technique embodied in Jerome Berryman's groundbreaking Godly Play curriculum for children's catechesis. Each week we address four wonderings. The key to a wondering is that it draws out a person's experience and imagination: it's not fixated on a right answer, but dwells gently and playfully on each person's latent perception and insight. So, for example, if the subject for the week is the Bible, the wonderings might be as follows. 'I wonder if there's a story you've loved a long time.' 'I wonder if there's a story about your family that everyone's heard too many times.' 'I wonder if you've ever felt there was a story that had no place for you.' 'I wonder if you've ever felt there was a story that *did* have a place for you.' Not everyone has to respond to each of the wonderings. The point is to increase the sense of respectful playfulness, where each participant appreciates and builds on the contribution of the others, like a game of keepy-uppy where a circle of people try to keep a soccer ball in the air without using their hands. When it goes well, you can feel people inspired by discovering things about themselves, as well as growing in wonder as others disclose humour, wisdom and surprises.

After about 40 minutes of such exploration and offering, it's time for the leader to speak about one place of wisdom in the Christian tradition. Let's say it's the Bible again. The leader weaves together the insights shared among the participants, highlighting places where the experience named resonates with a key theme to be communicated. So let's say the leader describes the Bible as like a five-act play, with creation, covenant, Christ, church and consummation. Talking about act five, consummation, the leader says that this is what it's like to be in a story that *does* have a place for us, a story where a kaleidoscope of identities and histories together make a gloriously diverse beauty. Likewise in act four, we get moments in our experience of church that thrillingly anticipate that embracing story, moments when we say the kingdom (or act five) breaks into act four. In act one, creation, God says to us, 'I made you this way because I wanted one like you,' and the leader can quote people's experience of what it's like to be excluded from a story when others don't know what to do with one like you. In act two, covenant, or the Old Testament, the leader can cite what participants have shared about being part of a community that constantly wonders if it has everything it needs and tells the same stories over and again.

Then finally, in the last half-hour, there's time for the participants to place what the leader has said side by side with their experience, shared or withheld, so each can evaluate this new information in the light of what they already live by. 'How does this fit?' says one; 'What do I do with my feelings about that?' says another. On one occasion, a participant digested an account of Christ's death drawn out of his own experience of being with and being alone, God's presence and absence, and the way Christ's spreadeagled hands are saying, 'I have set you as a seal upon my arm, to show you love is stronger than death.' Pondering the narrowness of what he had been told about the cross a decade earlier, and the expansiveness of this new perspective, he broke down in front of the group and said, 'Why did no one tell me this before?' The truth is, no one could have, if they had not first listened to his life experience and enabled him to fold those insights together with Christ's story like two climbing vines interweaving with one another.

It was at this point, towards the end of the last session together, that one participant, despite having joined energetically in the course, voiced her disappointment. 'When,' she said, 'are we going to talk about the Holy Spirit?' It wasn't immediately clear to Sam what the question was precisely referring to, but Sally quickly understood. Some enquirers' courses centre on a weekend away where participants invariably have an experience of a strange and wonderful warming of the heart and a new intimacy with God. We hadn't done this together on our course, and this participant was feeling short-changed, as it emerged a close friend of hers had been involved with a church where such experiences were common. When Sam appreciated what the question meant, he quickly realized what the answer was. It became the focal moment of the whole ten-week course, the big reveal that until that instant we hadn't at all identified as a big reveal.

He said, 'This *whole course* has been about the Holy Spirit. A Holy Spirit who's been acting in your life since the day you were born, a Holy Spirit who's made Christ present to you in friend and stranger, a Holy Spirit who's bestowed on you gifts of love, joy and peace, patience, faithfulness and gentleness. This whole course has been tracing how God has been speaking to you all along, how the work of the Holy Spirit in making Christ present is by no means restricted to the church but is revealed in every instance where the kingdom breaks in through acts of generosity, reconciliation and grace. What we've been modelling together is a way of discerning the work and voice of the Holy Spirit, as we've explored our past experience and present imagination and discovered together wisdom and truth. What we've been doing is weaving together the two climbing vines of the Christian story and our story, till we realize we can't perceive one without the other. What we've discovered is not just the way the Holy Spirit breathes through the Bible, the Eucharist, prayer and baptism, but how the Holy Spirit humbles the Church by speaking through the stranger, the outcast, the overlooked and the lowly. Is there anything more wonderful, more life-changing than this?'

Just as we all know Mary's a Catholic, and the Bible belongs to those who put it in a leather-bound zip-around case, we all know the Holy Spirit belongs to the charismatics. But leaving Mary aside, if the mainline Church tries to live without the Bible and the Holy Spirit, it won't get very far because it's cutting off its oxygen supply. What the Church needs more than anything else is a renewed understanding of the Holy Spirit and how it works to transform church through kingdom and thus give us glimpses of for ever now.

One of Billy Joel's least tuneful but most memorable songs is called 'We didn't start the fire'. It details over a hundred historical events that took place from the date of his birth in 1949 to the date the song was written in 1989. The cumulative effect is to see how much momentous activity there has been around the world – and how little of it has been initiated or shaped by an ordinary American household. It's a song that demonstrates powerfully what Sam said falteringly to that enquirers' group participant who was hoping for some eye-catching manifestation of the Holy Spirit. The Holy Spirit is a fire. A church that tries to control it, whether through rigid liturgies at set service times in specific buildings or through specific dramatic experiences in carefully engineered contexts with a limited range of legitimate meanings, is trying to control a fire with a brick. We didn't start the fire. We don't get to direct the fire. We don't get to say what occurrences are triggered by the fire and what aren't.

Here's the crucial mistake we make about the Holy Spirit. We convince ourselves that the Spirit is in short supply. It's ours to distribute to people like us, and we don't have much to go round. We couldn't be more wrong. The Holy Spirit is working in every single person's life the world over, and is constantly bringing forth glimpses of God's glory, whether through outpourings of grace or realizations of wonder or moments of reconciliation. We didn't start the fire. We don't get to control the fire. But sometimes we feel it burning within us as friend or stranger reveals its work to us.

One of the greatest joys of lockdown is that we have discovered that the Holy Spirit has been working in the lives of people who have had little or no link to the Church. The Church is good at engaging with and receiving as gifts those who can make it to our buildings every week; we may even be fine at visiting and supporting those who attend church but then have to stop due to disability or ill health. However, we have missed the gifts of those who have been housebound for a long time. The third time we led this course we advertised it through our Morning Prayer service, which by this point was entirely online. The third group we led had a significant number of people who were unable regularly to attend a local church due to disability, ill health or other reasons. It was as if they had been waiting to find each other and to find us and to explore faith together. What they discovered was that they didn't need to attend our buildings to find God, but that God had been with them, in their homes, all along. As they brought their experiences and reflections to the group, we all glimpsed the truth, beauty and goodness of God. We (Sally and Sam) were led somewhere we had not entirely planned, led to see our faith from a new angle and discover new perspectives on Christ.

A former teacher of Sam's spent a season serving a church in Ghana. Ghana gets very hot in the summer, and there is not much by way of air conditioning. Her church didn't have enough money to put glass in the windows. The good side of that was that it let a bit of air in. The bad side was that there was also quite a strong breeze. When they brought papers into the church for music or preaching or announcements the papers blew all around everywhere. Eventually they decided that having the wind blowing through the church was intolerable. So they got together enough money to put glass in all the windows. The result was simple. The wind blew the roof off.

That's how much the Spirit wants to bring us into relationship with God in Christ. That's what happens to the Church if it doesn't learn to enjoy the ways of the Spirit. Here's what Sam wishes he had said to that disappointed member of the enquirers' course. 'Treat every person you meet as one through whom the Spirit is communicating Christ to you. Treat every experience of your life as one in which the Spirit is longing to break through to you. Here's your choice: warm yourself by the Spirit's fire, or, if you don't – sooner or later, God's gonna blow your roof off, too.'

Conclusion

A Strategy for Transformation

SALLY HITCHINER

Apparently, if you want to improve your mental health during a pandemic, one approach is to start watching films about the apocalypse. All films in the genre, from zombies to tidal waves, seem to have this effect; but films about pandemics seem particularly potent.[1] Perhaps it's the escapism. But I wonder if it's more than this. Sam Wells voiced it, saying quite a few times that the challenge of living where we live now, facing what we face now, is that we don't know where we fit into this story. We don't know if it's the beginning, middle or end. In March 2020 there were those who believed that we were one-third of the way through the story, that we would have a month, maybe six weeks of lockdown, then the pandemic would be over and we could all go back to normal life. It seems naive now, but it wasn't so strange then. Even now as I write in November 2020, it's easy to hope that we are towards the end of things, when in all likelihood we're still in the early chapters. We don't know how it will play out. We don't know what will be needed of us. Most people who have not lived through extreme suffering are used to knowing the path of their lives. The liminal moments we have experienced – leaving home, going to university, changing jobs or moving cities – have well-worn narratives, rites of passage even, roadmaps of what to expect, discoverable with any quick google.

---

1 Ian Sample, 'I feel fine: fans of world-ending films "coping better with pandemic"', *The Guardian*, 1 July 2020, www.theguardian.com/science/2020/jul/01/end-of-the-world-as-we-know-it-fans-of-apocalyptic-films?CMP=Share_iOSApp_Other, accessed 30.11.2020.

How does one form a strategy for a church or any other organization at a time like this? How does one decide how best to use our resources, when to act, when to hold still? I'd like to offer a few thoughts that have helped us over recent months, that may be helpful in discerning ways forward in diverse settings.

You are now liminal

The first realization was that we are not in normal time. It sounds obvious, but the recognition that we are outside the established laws of how to act and what to do was liberating. A pandemic is a liminal space of epic proportions. I would repeat this to myself over and over: it shouldn't be the pressure of accomplishing the same as we did before but neither should it be the paralysis of not knowing anything – we are in a different time. A liminal time can be similar to the experience of a new job. It's OK for us to take time to adjust, but neither should we cocoon until life returns to something we recognize. Much has been written about liminal spaces over the past 100 years. This is an area we know about. We have something of a map available – albeit a sketchy pictorial one, rather than to scale and entirely reliable. Spaces that are between are a mixture of areas with well-established expectations and behaviours; airport lounges, teenage years, text messages or the office party are disconcerting, because they are in-between areas of accepted norms. They are a mixture of zones, a mixture of more than one, or outside the boundaries of sets of established social rules. Everyone knows how to act at a work meeting – what to wear, what you drink. Everyone knows how to act at home – what you wear, what you eat or drink. A Zoom meeting from your home is a mixture of worlds. Which rules do you follow? Is it acceptable to bring your breakfast to a meeting? A glass of wine? Are T-shirts acceptable for an internal meeting? What about a meeting with an external client? The rules are no longer clear, but unlike a new job, the rules are not clear to anyone – anyone in the world. And if those rules are no longer clear to anyone, there is a window where the rules can be moveable in a liminal time. In a pandemic there is no moral autopilot. But we are not without compass and guide.

Don't plan for a crisis

Yes, you read that right. The thing we have learned at St Martin's about strategy for a pandemic is – don't strategize for a pandemic. For something that has actually been long anticipated, it's surprising how hard it was to predict anything of use. The Diocese of London planned for a pandemic. The Diocese of London planned for up to 20 per cent of priests to be unable to function. What they didn't plan for was a full lockdown of *all* churches at once. Even with access to the greatest strategy experts in the world, the UK government (and the opposition) was having to feel its way through the early stages of the 2020 pandemic. However important crisis tabletop exercises can be, the likelihood is that the reality will be entirely different from what was planned.

Sam Wells holds that the problem with much thought about ethics – or to put it another way, the way we live – is that we focus too much on the crisis. In crisis, human beings only ever do what they have always done. If we have grown habits of generosity or selfishness, of honesty or deception, this is what will come out in a crisis. 'The battle of Waterloo was won on the playing fields of Eton,' said the Duke of Wellington, intending not to boast about his education, but to say that entrenched habits come out when we are under pressure. We show our true colours. So why not focus on those in deciding how we want to live every day, not just in the crisis? The real value in tabletop exercises is not that they create new ways of working but that they enable old cultures *to keep working* in the midst of new situations. The question about how to respond in a crisis is best responded to with the question of how to live well in everyday life. Then the crisis won't seem so much of a crisis … it will seem obvious to you how to act: you've always acted like this. A crisis is just a megaphone for how we live every day.

There is a deep-set culture in St Martin's of thinking about how to ensure that every member of our congregation is able to access our church life, and of going the extra mile to make sure we don't lose those members of our community with access needs around disability. This isn't an act of kindness towards those who are excluded; it is an indication of the need we each have for the other. So in February 2020, prior to the first lockdown, when some members of our community started self-isolating due to physical vulnerabilities, we explored whether we could livestream services using our mobile phones so we didn't have to lose them from our worship. It was just a whim; we wondered if it would work. I set up my mobile phone one morning, without any big announcement or advertising, and livestreamed our service of Morning Prayer to our congregation Facebook page. Sixty people saw what we were doing and stayed to pray with us for the service. During the subsequent 24 hours, over 1,000 people watched some of it. Most of those who joined us were not our regular congregation; and we suspect that a lot were not regular churchgoers at all. I wished I'd thought to dress up a little more. We stumbled upon online worship, not because we were trying to be novel, but because we were practising an old habit of ensuring access for each member of our community.

We have all the time in the world

Again, this may seem like a strange thing to read in a chapter on how to form a strategy in a pandemic. And yet, this is one of the most important things we need in the middle of a crisis. I rediscovered Louis Armstrong singing this while walking through the sunshine of a deserted central London and had it on repeat, humming it to myself for about a week. 'We have all the time in the world ... just for love.'[2]

---

2 Composed by John Barry, lyrics by Hal David, 'All the Time in the World' (1963) from the album *On Her Majesty's Secret Service*, EMI Records Ltd.

In a crisis the pressure to flee until things return to normal, or fight to prevent things from changing, or to fix things back to normal as quickly as possible, is enormous. However, there is only one direction in a crisis: forwards. The anthropologist Victor Turner noted that there are three stages to the experience of liminality. The individual is separated from the old; they exist in the liminal space and in doing this are changed; then they are reintegrated into society again as a new version of themselves. Going backwards isn't an option; rushing doesn't get you anywhere. The only way is forwards, and the only way to progress is to make your peace with the stage you're in right now. When the whole world is going through a pandemic, the only thing you can be sure of is that the new world will be different. Going forward through these phases, making our peace with them and baptizing them as we go, is the only strategy for us.

Shortly before the pandemic started, we were trialling a new course, outlined in Chapter 14 above. One of the groups Sam and I were leading over much of the first lockdown had a significant number of participants whose lives hadn't been all they had hoped due to illness or disability. One session we were talking about eternal life, and the penny dropped. What if this life isn't your only shot? What if we can try things we've missed out on later? You could see the hope begin to burst on their faces as they voiced this.

It rests not on an observation of the world, but on belief in God. What if God has enough for us to follow Christ and to be reconciled with ourselves, each other and the world? What if God really is generous? If there really is all the time in the world (and the next world), if God in Christ has already done the work of saving the world, and if the work of fixing the world and broken lives so they reflect this belongs with God and will be culminated in Christ's return, then our work here becomes less pressured. We are invited to have a go at living in the characteristics of Christ. We are invited to join with God in this work without the pressure that it all depends on us. Creating space where communities can experiment together is key to this.

Build playgrounds

I seem to be making a habit of writing section headings that seem a little strange in books about pandemics. The good news is that a liminal space is packed full of all sorts of possibilities you wouldn't find in everyday life. If you want to write a romance novel, set the opening of the story in an airport departure lounge on Christmas Eve or a lift that gets stuck between floors or a beach resort in February, and half the work is done for you. People in liminal spaces do things they wouldn't normally do. They can explore a side of themselves they had forgotten about or didn't think they were capable of. It's also true for the expectations of others on an individual. Think of the experience of women in the workplace in the 1940s. Can you imagine women being so depended upon for thought and expertise, let alone manual labour, without a world war?

St Martin's is rooted in a belief that God provides us with everything we need to follow Christ together, but that this might come from unexpected sources. We needed a space to share and hear with as many of our community as possible. There were no perfect platforms, so we landed on Facebook. At the time of writing, Facebook is popular with neither older members of our congregation nor younger ones. But it had something we needed and couldn't find on other platforms. As we set up the online spaces for worship, we also created a congregational Facebook page, set up so that only those who are on the electoral roll can see what is posted, a safe space to try new ideas and share information that they wouldn't want to share more widely. Anyone could have an idea for providing pastoral, community or spiritual growth through the lockdown and try it out. If it didn't work, it was no big deal.

One of our congregation, in spite of a deep faith, has always held back from opportunities to speak or lead. However, faced with the needs of the pandemic, where we were all out of our depth, they started posting daily Lectio Divina, encouraging others to reflect on the day's reading with them. This has been one of the most significant parts of our daily community life. Others have discovered a new gift for leading Compline services, or online baking workshops or exercise classes. We couldn't have predicted what was needed over this year, but by creating space for ideas to be tried out, and space for the whole community to share, we broaden the possibility that we can discover solutions together. What we are finding, in all our different platforms, is that in the word 'together' lies the solution.

Ritual

Liminality suits some people more than others. For those who have been treated well by the established rules, who have found it easy to access society and progress up the hierarchies, a liminal space can feel disruptive and confusing. It can take longer to process what is happening. But most of us are used to having some sense of choice over our own lives. Whatever the rights and wrongs of it, we are people who are used to choice: so let our choices be towards Christ. The Benedictine Rule of Life prioritizes daily conversion. I wonder if this is linked to the history of the Benedictines being more rooted in the establishment than the Franciscans or some other orders. A new day, let alone a new experience of life, needs a new conversion commitment. Large changes in life can throw our faith. It is quite common for someone to be a weekly church attender as a teenager but not attend church at university, until it comes to the holidays, when they return home, and wouldn't miss it. Their new paradigm isn't yet Christian.

One of the things that can help everyone following a large change is ritual. A meaningful vocalization or enactment of the new reality can be powerful in itself. This new life may be scary and confusing, but if we are understood we are not alone, and if we are not alone, that makes all the difference in the world. When you combine this with a meaningful assertion that God has a history of caring for people in situations like ours, that God cares for us now and is with us here, ritual can be life-changing.

We went into a full lockdown in March, but by Easter morning we found ourselves in an explosion of energy and creativity.

The dawn service started with me carrying a small candle from the church to the vicarage. The service built and built until the moment when Christ rose from the dead and we flung open the windows, ringing bells and popping party poppers. Writing this down, it strikes me that this is what many churches do every year for the Easter dawn service, St Martin's included. But this year it had an explosiveness that seemed to mirror our experience of life at that time. We were looking for liturgy and drama to engage with our reality. We were looking for liminal rites. And it helped. Afterwards, buzzing with excitement, it felt important to have enacted this in this way. The greatest event in our lives, even at that time, was not the pandemic. The most influential act on the world, even then, was not Covid. There was something more explosive.

Whether it is a service to celebrate an adoption, or a graduation, a ceremony to acknowledge a divorce or a rupture in a community, rites create their own liminal space. In the words of the Eucharist, these liminal rites take, bless, break and give back something, someone new to the community.

Invest in relationships

The people who told you that 'life is a marathon, not a sprint' only told you half the story. True, it is a long race; but what we have found over the pandemic is that pacing yourself doesn't give you all the answers. One of the greatest lessons we have learned is to act like an improvisation troupe, like relay runners, as a team.

Richard Carter and I were the first members of the team to throw ourselves into reimagining church life in this new world. We quickly set up livestreaming of services. Richard responded to the increasing numbers of people who found themselves homeless on Trafalgar Square. I set up community spaces online and encouraged congregation-led initiatives within them. Richard divided up the elderly members of our congregation so that each would get a regular phone call from a priest, and I set up a system of congregation-led micro-group care called our Faith Companions, where most of the congregation formed cross-generational hubs of three or four people, promising to make contact with one another each week. We had the active support of our colleagues, but Richard and I look back on this time and wonder why it was us who ended up with the energy to lead the initial surge. We wonder if it is because both of us, in different ways, have lived with liminality more than perhaps our colleagues. I grew up with middle-class parents in a working-class environment. Richard spent ten years as a chaplain and brother of a monastic community in Melanesia. I spent seven years as a university chaplain in an institution without a well-established role for this. Richard has spent his life with those on the edges. We wonder if our comfortableness with the strangeness of the early stages of the pandemic was linked to the fact that, to one degree or another, we have always lived in strangeness. We learned the craft of priesthood not in stability and accepted patterns but in internal and external liminality. To be in an extremely liminal space felt exhilarating.

However, this gift had its limits. A few months in, new challenges hit. How could we support our business, our congregation and our community as they emerged from the first lockdown? Unsurprisingly, Richard and I were tired. 'I feel tired in my bones,' Richard said to me one day. We managed to take holidays, but it took months to recover. If it had been down to us, church would have stopped mid-June. Just at the right moment, the lockdown lifted, other members of the clergy who hadn't found the initial stages so invigorating or lived too far away to be on-site for the lockdown, now stepped up in their moment to lead. They had insights, energy and vision for new challenges. I was able to move into a support role and coast behind other people's good ideas and strength. Being a priest isn't about leading everything. I've seen this same story play out whether it is between clergy or laity or a mixture of both. We are increasing the responsibilities of our PCC this year to recognize this. We need a team to lead a church through a pandemic.

Of course, we have our fair share of pulling our hair out with each other, and I think it's a pretty safe bet that my colleagues do about me, even if they are too polite to put it in a book. But then, two weeks or two months later, they'll do something that only they could do, and I find myself in a situation where I'm thinking, 'How on earth could we have survived this without you?' The next time I'm frustrated that they're not like me, I remember this occasion, and it dampens the frustration. God gives us everything we need to follow Christ. But it's never just in one person's pockets. You don't need me to tell you why a God of love might arrange it this way.

Eat together

The year before the pandemic the clergy team started having meals together once a term, taking turns to host. The first time it felt awkward; the second time a little less so. By the third time we were relaxed and comfortable with each other and we actively enjoyed each other's company. The challenge of being in a broad church is that 'complementarity' seems like a dirty word. It has too often been used to oppress women, to exclude, to limit the possibilities of church and keep people in their 'place'. The challenge in less conservative churches is that we can end up believing (or at least acting as if we believe) that all priests have to be equally good at everything. There is little room for an individual to be individual or for a team of people to discover the beauty of a rainbow of skill sets among them.

We discover this way of being most readily when we step aside from settings where there is an obvious goal in mind. In a social occasion we have the opportunity to drop the desire to use people and instead to enjoy each other. We get used to some members of the group being lively conversationists and others gentle listeners. Some always bring excellent bottles of wine, others make the most delicious desserts. We notice what people give, rather than what they lack. It's hard to have a ruthlessly utilitarian perspective on people you eat with. This, in my view, changed how we responded to the pandemic.

I once worked briefly with Justin Welby. Before he became Archbishop of Canterbury, he was Canon for Reconciliation at Coventry Cathedral. Part of this involved risking his life to go into situations of conflict and war. I wanted to know how he worked with terrorists. I don't think I'll ever forget his answer. He said that you go into your first meeting with them with only one objective: to find something you genuinely like about them. 'You can't fake it,' he said. 'They may be a terrible person, but if they are decent to their secretary or a doting grandfather you have something you can work with.' I should point out that my colleagues are a long way from terrorists, even on a bad day. But this principle is universal. We can only work with each other as Christians if we view each other's gifts before our limitations. It works because this is the way God sees us.

Ready Steady Cook

In the 1990s and 2000s there was a popular British TV show called *Ready Steady Cook*. The premise was that participants bring in a bag of mystery ingredients and give a brief to two chefs: 'I'd like something to remind me of my holiday in Sardinia,' or 'I've never known how to cook with aubergine, so I've brought in some strawberries and chicken stock to see how they could be combined.' The chefs are then against the clock to create a delicious meal showcasing the ingredients, using only basic additions from their kitchen cupboards. Leading in the pandemic can feel a little like this, with new announcements from the government every few weeks, sometimes every few days, to throw a spanner in the works. It was never going to be an easy task. Steps forward are often stumbled upon, and mistakes are to be expected. Leaders need to be given space in a pandemic to realize that results are not a measure of who they are.

But by understanding something of the nature of liminal times, investing in relationships, relying on team, communicating, being present where we can, and ultimately by falling back on key values that we invest in year after year, we have ingredients that can transform our experience and that of our community. We cannot fix the pandemic. But we can find God, ourselves, and each other in the middle of it. And with this, we discover not the achievement, but the gift, of being church.

Epilogue

Being Church in a Global Pandemic

SAMUEL WELLS

I don't believe the pandemic has introduced any particular new theological truth. But I do believe it has been a refiner's fire that has revealed a number of dynamics that were previously much more hidden, and that there are ways we can distinguish Before Covid, BC, from After Covid, AC.

AC, I see a humbler Church with a bigger God. I want to explain what I mean by that. The French Jesuit Michel de Certeau distinguishes between a strategy and a tactic. A strategy builds a citadel, and from its control base makes forays into the hinterland. A tactic has no home base, nowhere to store its booty, and survives by hand-to-hand encounters on the ground. I want to put these contrasting concepts to use with a broad distinction.

Here are two familiar sentiments. 'Make me a channel of your peace', says the 1967 hymn based on a prayer written in France in 1912 and widely, though mistakenly, attributed to St Francis. 'Christ has no body now but yours. No hands, no feet on earth but yours.' So says the sixteenth-century Spanish mystic Teresa of Avila. I want to highlight what these two sentiments have in common. They assume what I'm going to call a strategy church. A strategy church makes two assumptions that I think are relevant to our BC/AC discussion. The first is an unspoken sense that Jesus ascended before he had actually finished his work among us, and that therefore it falls to us, his beloved and chosen followers, to complete the work he was too busy or distracted to attend to. The second is that if one imagines an hourglass, with the top and much larger part being heaven and the bottom and smaller part being earthly existence, and Jesus being the aperture through which the angels ascend and descend between the two, then we, or more precisely the Church, currently constitute that aperture. The Church is the principal and definitive way in which God continues to work in the world after the manner of Christ's incarnation.

Now let me contrast this picture with what I'm going to call tactic church. 'Christ plays in ten thousand places,' says another Jesuit, Gerard Manley Hopkins. 'Lovely in limbs, and lovely in eyes not his.' Notice how this tactic language differs from the assumptions of a strategy church. A colleague told me about three women who attended a church BC. The church had to shut for a few weeks for repairs. So the three women made a plan. One went to car boot sales each Sunday morning, met and talked to the regulars, formed relationships and learned much. Another went to Sunday league football games and had a similar experience. A third went to an Ikea store and got to know staff and customers. After a few weeks, the three women compared notes, and had enough information to become excited about what they were discovering and understanding. When the time came for the church to reopen after the refit, they had a genuine quandary about whether to return or whether to continue in their explorations. One of them explained, 'Our God is now too big to fit back into our church.' What they were naming was their discovery of tactic church. Tactic church does not assume everything God is doing comes through the church. It doesn't assume the best example of God's ways is always the church. It rejoices to discover the surprises of what the Spirit is doing in unexpected places through unheralded people. Tactic church entails a humbler church; but apprehends a bigger God.

What I'm describing imitates the transformation described in second Isaiah. In exile, beleaguered and bereft, Israel learned that its God was a much bigger God – the God of the whole world. But it also learned that God was more than happy to use agents other than itself, such as Cyrus, who didn't even claim to know Israel's God. That's the discovery we now need to recall.

The pandemic has so far had three key phases with different characteristics, each of which has proved a litmus test for the Church. The first phase was a rapid, collective confrontation with mortality. A culture that has largely succeeded in its project of denying, delaying and distracting from death suddenly had to face the prospect of mass mortality. While that prospect didn't fully materialize, the litmus test for the Church was, 'Is the Church a reliable, gentle and trustworthy presence in the face of death?' The final test of a friend is, 'Would I want you beside me on my deathbed?' The point is not fundamentally about whether churches were open or not. It's about whether, in the face of the world's preoccupations and the Church's obsessions, the Church was able to show its true colours when the whole country was confronted with fear, isolation, grief, powerlessness and despair. If so, it proved itself a true companion to the nation. If not, it failed at its moment of greatest possibility.

The second phase, stretching from the easing of lockdown to the introduction of the tier system, was characterized by exasperation, confusion and hardship. While the most important thing in ministry is to be with people in the most challenging moments of their lives, most of all as they face death, the most frequent calling of ministry is to be an abiding presence as people address, over the long term, problems that won't go away, situations for which there is no quick fix, and issues that leave them feeling powerless. Some of this ministry is exercised by simply paying sustained attention; some by entering with people deeper into the mystery than they could dare to go alone; some again by renarrating their experience as part of a larger story. Whichever it is, the key question remains: 'Has the Church proved itself to be a good companion in uncertain and troubling times, not eager to find a false solution or collude in the culture of anger and blame?'

When you have been through a crisis with someone, you may return to a previous level of relationship, but you never forget what you discovered about that person and about your relationship in that intense time. What we're experiencing is not something that is primarily or fundamentally happening to the Church; it's something that is almost uniquely happening to the whole world, and the Church's true colours are being revealed by whether it has been able to face the challenge on the one hand of mortality and on the other hand of extended uncertainty and dislocation. This should be the Church's natural habitat. After all, death and resurrection are the epicentre of Christianity, and Egypt and Babylon, the locations of extended discomfort and dislocation, are the crucible of the Old Testament, where God was made known like no other moment. If there has been anger and blame, it has arisen out of clergy and laypeople's feelings of irrelevance and powerlessness – feelings that no amount of home food delivery or frenetic online communication can alleviate. These feelings of irrelevance and powerlessness are not to be brushed aside or regarded as signs of immaturity. They can be a stimulus to rediscover a tactic church when the strategy church is no longer fit for purpose.

The third phase, which we are still in, began with the tier system and stretched into further lockdown, but is different because we now have the prospect of the pandemic coming to an end. Originally we imagined it would peter out. Then we thought we could contain it. Now we believe the cavalry are coming in the shape of a vaccine. This period is characterized by patience. It's an Advent season. Advent is perhaps the most distinctive Christian season of all. We find ourselves in between the coming of Christ as a baby and his return in glory. We have to remind ourselves that we're at a particular place in a story. Ruth had many travails: but she takes her place in the story of Israel. Rahab had a complex life: but she lines up in the genealogy of Jesus. We struggle today; but we too are folded into God's story. It's better to fail in a cause that will finally succeed than to succeed in a cause that will finally fail. That's the message of Advent. And it pinches particularly in an era when the Church seems to be on the back foot, and visible signs of being on the right side of history seem few. It's hard to wait with patience when the clouds seem dark. But this is the heart of pastoral care – to be with people when all seems bleak, and trust that God will never depart and goodness will prevail.

Sometimes we need to adjust the timescale, but nothing bad lasts for ever. Our lives are hid with Christ in God.

We can put a lot of energy into taking church online, and it can do a lot of good in reimagining and re-evaluating what we do and why. We can make education, board meetings, synods and international links so much cheaper, more nimble and less cumbersome by removing the labour of travel and hospitality. All these things can change the shape of the Church. But these changes are superficial if they are not grounded in a renewal of our calling to be with people facing mortality, living with uncertainty and waiting with patience. Those who are wearied by the changes and chances of this fleeting world should find in us sure and certain hope of God's eternal changelessness.

The transformation from being a strategy church to being a tactic church isn't a downgrade, a downsize, or what is today euphemistically known as a restructure. Its success isn't to be judged by the number of hits on YouTube or the quantity of column inches in the national press that no one reads any more but everyone still wants to be quoted in. Christianity isn't a popularity contest where getting a lot of retweets gets us nearer to the kingdom. It's an encounter with truth, to the bottom of our souls and to the very heart of God. The pandemic has been a complete nightmare, but it can still be a gift, if it restores our clarity about our core purpose: to be with people in the night-time of their fear, with faith, hope and love in the God who, in Christ, heals our past and frees our future.

Contributors

Richard Carter is Associate Vicar for Mission at St Martin-in-the-Fields and leader of the Nazareth Community. He is the author of *The City is My Monastery: A Contemporary Rule of Life* (Norwich: Canterbury Press, 2019).

Harry Ching is Assistant Vicar for International Ministry and priest to the Chinese congregation at St Martin-in-the-Fields. He previously served in Cyprus and the United Arab Emirates in the Diocese of Cyprus and the Gulf.

Catherine Duce is Assistant Vicar for Partnership Development at St Martin-in-the-Fields. She has a background in theological action research and spends her time growing HeartEdge in London as a member of the Nazareth Community.

Andrew Earis is Director of Music of St Martin-in-the-Fields, where he oversees the busy music in worship, culture and concert programmes. He is also a producer of BBC Radio religious worship, and works closely with the Church of England on their online church music output.

Jonathan Evens is Associate Vicar for HeartEdge at St Martin-in-the-Fields and Chair of Churches Together in Westminster. He writes regularly on the visual arts and co-authored *The Secret Chord*, a study of faith and pop music.

Sally Hitchiner is Associate Vicar for Ministry at St Martin-in-the-Fields. She speaks regularly in the national media on issues of faith, ethics and contemporary culture.

Fiona MacMillan is chair of the Disability Advisory Group at St Martin-in-the-Fields and a trustee of Inclusive Church. She is known for knitting together lived experience, creative connections and questions of social justice.

Andy Turner is HeartEdge Development Coordinator. He lives in east London.

Samuel Wells is Vicar of St Martin-in-the-Fields and Visiting Professor of Christian Ethics at King's College London. He is the author of many books, including *Walk Humbly* (Norwich: Canterbury Press, 2019) and *Love Mercy* (Norwich: Canterbury Press, 2020).

CPSIA information can be obtained
at www.ICGtesting.com
Printed in the USA
LVHW112020310521
688959LV00001B/1